W9-CUX-286

Agamid Lizards

ULRICH MANTHEY AND NORBERT SCHUSTER

TRANSLATOR: WILLIAM CHARLTON

Originally published in German under the title *Agamen* by Terrarien Bibliothek. ©1992 by Herpetologischer Fachverlag Ralf Heselhaus and Matthias Schmidt GBR, Muenster.

Copyright ©1996 by T.F.H. Publications, Inc. for the English-language edition. A considerable amount of new material, including but not limited to additional photographs, has been added to this English-language edition. Copyright is also claimed for this new material.

© 1996 by T.F.H. Publications, Inc.

Distributed in the UNITED STATES to the Pet Trade by T.F.H. Publications, Inc., One T.F.H. Plaza, Neptune City, NJ 07753; distributed in the UNITED STATES to the Bookstore and Library Trade by National Book Network, Inc. 4720 Boston Way, Lanham MD 20706; in CANADA to the Pet Trade by H & L Pet Supplies Inc., 27 Kingston Crescent, Kitchener, Ontario N2B 2T6; Rolf C. Hagen Inc., 3225 Sartelon St. Laurent-Montreal Quebec H4R 1E8; in CANADA to the Book Trade by Vanwell Publishing Ltd., 1 Northrup Crescent, St. Catharines, Ontario L2M 6P5 ; in ENGLAND by T.F.H. Publications, PO Box 15, Waterlooville PO7 6BQ; in AUSTRALIA AND THE SOUTH PACIFIC by T.F.H. (Australia), Pty. Ltd., Box 149, Brookvale 2100 N.S.W., Australia; in NEW ZEALAND by Brooklands Aquarium Ltd. 5 McGiven Drive, New Plymouth, RD1 New Zealand; in Japan by T.F.H. Publications, Japan—Jiro Tsuda, 10-12-3 Ohjidai, Sakura, Chiba 285, Japan; in SOUTH AFRICA by Lopis (Pty) Ltd., P.O. Box 39127, Booysens, 2016, Johannesburg, South Africa. Published by T.F.H. Publications, Inc.
MANUFACTURED IN THE
UNITED STATES OF AMERICA
BY T.F.H. PUBLICATIONS, INC.

Contents

Foreword

Although agamids form an extremely peculiar and variable family and numerous species are kept in captivity, up to now they have been badly neglected in the terrarium literature. The aim of this book is to reduce the information deficit and to provide an initial overview. Our intention is not to offer a recipe book according to the motto: "You take (*fill in the blank*). . . and obtain healthy lizards with numerous offspring." The subject is much too complex for that. Moreover, no information at all exists on the behavior of many species. Rather, we want to communicate our experiences in the terrarium hobby and supplement them with field observations. However, we do not wish to hide the fact that we were also dependent on the assistance of other hobbyists and scientists.

The numerous breeding successes in recent years demonstrate emphatically the high level attained by the present-day terrarium hobby. Unfortunately, the successes have also been accompanied by failures, the number of which must be reduced. Through keeping animals in terraria we gain insight into the behavior of many species in which long-term studies are scarcely practical. Nevertheless, it is impossible to duplicate all of the natural factors that affect the life of a lizard, such as climate, predators, territory size, and range of foods, in the terrarium. Therefore, the findings gained in the terrarium hobby must also be viewed with a certain amount of skepticism. They can supplement studies in the wild, but not replace them.

If this book helps to bring the beginner closer to the bizarre world of the agamids and also offers something new to the experienced hobbyist, then our goal will have been achieved.

Berlin/Darmstadt
Ulrich Manthey, Norbert Schuster

Acknowledgments

We wish to give our heartfelt thanks to all those who gave us so much help, especially U. Bott, Bonn; J. Henkel, J. Lowewen, and S. Porcu, all from Darmstadt; as well as M. Bartz and W. Denzer, both from Berlin; Dr. U. Joger, Dieburg; A. Manning, Australia; J. Nabhitabhata, Thailand; and C. Steiof and F. Tillak, both from Berlin. Special thanks are due to our wives— Sybille, for the time-consuming corrections as well as her participation in the often exhausting excursions; and Ursel, for the care of the agamids.

Last but not least we thank the publisher for the always trusting and constructive cooperation.

Abbreviations

HBL—Head-body length, from tip
    of snout to posterior edge of
    vent
TL—Tail length
H—Height
L—Length
D—Width

Agamids, such as this striking male *Agama* sp. from Kilembe, Uganda, unfortunately have been neglected in the American segment of the terrarium hobby. Photo: M. Smith.

Introduction

Through foreign tourism and expanding international trade, lizard species are obtainable today for the terrarium hobby whose biology is still virtually unknown. In recent years agamids from the Indonesian region have been imported with some regularity for the first time, and in the near future lizards are also to be expected from those Asian countries that have only recently opened their borders. To provide a complete overview, all genera are presented. Also of decisive importance in this regard are comprehensive systematic works from the recent past, combined with numerous changes in the generic names, which were quite confusing in the case of the Australian agamids. The index at the end of the book makes it easier to find the individual species if they have changed genera.

The species grouped in a genus are not only similar in appearance, but in many cases they differ little from one another in their behavior and their dietary requirements. For this reason, and to keep repetition to a minimum, we have, for example, often supplied recommendations for keeping in the terrarium only in the generic description. Any special features that differ from the norm are mentioned under the individual species. Likewise, with the agamids that primarily feed on insects, we have avoided listing each time the entire identical palette of foods they consume, such as spiders or small invertebrates. The general section, however, contains sufficient information on diet as well as tips for setting up and furnishing the terrarium. The introductory chapters were intentionally shortened to make it possible to present more species, including a number of presently rarely seen forms.

The care of lizards, besides requiring a large portion of "intuition," also carries with it the responsibility for the creature's life. Therefore, it is essential to strive for keeping methods that are appropriate for the species and, if possible, directed toward breeding.

A gravid female Ground Agama, *Agama aculeata*, from Gemsbok Park, Kalahari, South Africa. Photo: K. H. Switak.

The Family Agamidae

SYSTEMATICS

The term *systematics* refers to the study of the relationships and history of species. *Taxonomy*, on the other hand, is the theory and practice of the *classification* of organisms. The subject matter of the two concepts partially overlaps. On the one hand, *classification* identifies results of taxonomy, and on the other it describes classification itself: "Zoological classification is the arranging of animals into groups on the basis of their similarity and kinship" (Mayr).

Systematics uses comparisons to study the special features that are shared by each species and each higher taxon (taxon = taxonomic group of whatever rank—species, genus, family, and so forth—that is different enough that the inclusion in a particular category seems justified; plural: taxa). Furthermore, the causes for variation in common characters are studied. The species is the lowest taxon and simultaneously the only one that is defined objectively: "Species are groups of

Agamids look much like iguanid lizards from the New World but often tend to have high spiny nape crests and more contrasting colors. Photo of a striking male *Calotes versicolor* by R. Heselhaus.

naturally interbreeding populations, which are reproductively isolated from other groups of that kind" (Mayr).

The father of modern taxonomy is considered to be the Swedish naturalist Linnaeus (1707-1778). In the tenth edition of his *Systema Naturae* (1758) he first used binomial nomenclature uniformly for the whole animal kingdom. (Binomial nomenclature involves the use of two Latinized names, the genus and the species, to consistently identify or name all living organisms.) The following century was characterized by the continual introduction of newly developed systems to express relationships, which, however, were unable to gain acceptance. Darwin (1809-1882) was the first to succeed, through his evolutionary explanations, in discovering the kindred relationships: "Natural" groups exist because the members of such a group descended from a common ancestor. This also created the foundation for modern systematics.

Despite the most modern methods of research, even today we still stand almost at the beginning with our knowledge of the kinship of certain groups of animals, so further divisions of genera and families will be unavoidable.

Literature: Ax, 1984; Mayr, 1975.

CLASSIFICATION OF THE AGAMIDS

The class of the reptiles (Reptilia) is divided into several orders. The true scaly reptiles (Squamata) make up one of them. It is divided into two suborders, snakes (Serpentes) and lizards (Sauria). The family Agamidae belongs to the latter.

The external appearance of the agamids resembles that of the iguanas, yet there does not seem to be a close relationship (Moody, 1980). With respect to the different forms of the teeth in agamids and iguanas, we need only to examine the molars. In agamids they are located precisely on the upper margin of the jaw (acrodont), and they are very strongly fused with the jaw and apparently also with the bases of adjacent teeth, so that a sawlike bony beak results. The loss of a tooth is final, since no new teeth grow back. In the iguanoids the teeth are distinct and set at the edge of the jaw (pleurodont).

If the uromastyx-like lizards (*Uromastyx* and *Leiolepis*) are considered to be a subfamily (Leiolepidinae) of the agamids, then we currently recognize about 340 species divided into 48 genera in the family Agamidae. The proposal that the chameleons and agamids share a family (Chamaeleonidae) is not accepted here.

A genus includes species that share either anatomic or morphologic (external) characters or at least have a combination of several characters in common. Quite a few agamids exhibit such a unique appearance or an unusual anatomy that only one species is known within a genus. The agamids include 18 of these monotypic genera, corresponding to about 38 percent of the total genera.

Literature: Ehmann, 1992; Leviton et al., 1992; Moody, 1980; Musters, 1983; Peters, 1984.

DISTRIBUTION

The agamids are the Old World counterparts of the New World iguanas and their relatives. The ranges of these groups (iguanas and their relatives currently are thought to represent several families in addition to the Iguanidae) do not overlap, if the exceptions on Fiji and Tonga in the Pacific and on Madagascar in the Indian Ocean are ignored. Agamids are found in Europe (Greece—several islands and introduced in several places on the mainland), Asia, Australia, part of the Pacific island world, and Africa. In several respects the African continent holds a special place. The agamids were unable to colonize the large island of Madagascar (iguanoids, however, are found there) off the African coast and they are absent from large parts of central Africa as well as the coastal strip of southwestern Africa. It is also worth noting that no typically arboreal (tree-climbing) agamids have evolved in Africa.

Through specialization the agamids have adapted to the most diverse climatic and faunal conditions. With the exception of the oceans, they inhabit all living spaces. They are present both in hot deserts and wet rainforests. An amazing achievement, and proof of their enormous adaptive capacity, is their occurrence at higher el-

Notice the large, high teeth of this *Agama* sp. from Uganda. Agamids have modified teeth fixed to the top of the jaw and developed as incisors, canines, and molars. Photo: M. Smith.

evations in the Himalayas (about 6000 meters). Even in summer, the temperature there may drop to -20°C and snow storms are not a rarity.

BIOLOGY

The generally diurnal (day-active) agamids have strongly developed limbs and five fingers and five toes (with the exception of *Sitana ponticeriana*) that are equipped with claws. The tail, which often cannot be regenerated, has evolved into a prehensile organ in several agamids. Many species are able to move their eyes independently of each other. In this way they are simultaneously able to see in different

Distribution of the Agamidae.

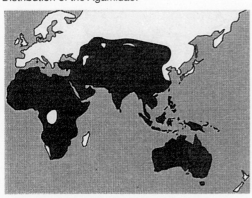

directions. They are usually incapable of producing vocalizations, but here too there are exceptions (for example, *Calotes emma*). The arrangement and appearance of the scales are very variable. In the same way as chameleons, many agamids can change their coloration and markings dramatically. Their body temperature is dependent on the ambient temperature (ectotherms). Changing the color and the position of the body, however, allows for a considerable regulation of the amount of heat collected during basking. The darkening of the skin, for example, enables the agamid to absorb warmth faster in the early morning hours. After the preferred temperature is reached, the skin turns lighter and then reflects a portion of the sunlight.

Desert-dwellers, in particular, are highly specialized so that they can survive under extreme climatic conditions. Some agamids, by means of indentations at the cloaca, reabsorb as much water as possible from the as yet unexcreted droppings. The salts dissolved in this water are excreted again by special glands in the nasal passages. Others take up water in form of dew and condensation through tiny channels in the skin and carry it to the mouth.

Sexual dimorphism is so pronounced

Many Asian agamids rarely are available and bring high prices when they appear on the market. One of the most bizarre and desirable is *Lyriocephalus scutatus*, the Lyre-headed Agamid of Sri Lanka. This is a female. Photo: Kielmann.

in a number of species that the females are more similar to female agamids of other species than they are to the males of their own species (for example, *Gonocephalus belli* and *Gonocephalus borneensis*). In others secondary sexual characters are absent.

Some agamids are unable to come into breeding condition without hibernation. The breeding season often is closely connected with the monsoon rains. During the breeding season the males court the females with a specific body language

and often coloration that are only exhibited during this time. Females of the same species are attracted in this way and stimulated to mate. A species-specific behavior of the female signals her readiness to breed. Before and during copulation the male bites the female's nape region or flanks.

As a rule, agamids lay eggs. They primarily lay their eggs in self-excavated holes, which they fill in again with the substrate in layers immediately afterward. To secure the individual layers of dirt sufficiently, many species use their head as a ram and thrust it at short intervals so vigorously against the ground that it is clearly audible even at a distance of several meters. Through the uptake of moisture, the more or less soft-shelled eggs increase in size and weight until the young hatch.

In general, the body build and other conspicuous external characters are indicative of the living space with some degree of certainty. Arboreal species have a laterally compressed body and additionally often are characterized by large throat fans (gular pouches) and dorsal crests.

Long hind legs indicate bipedal (two-legged) locomotion. On the other hand, short, very strong legs are splendidly suited for digging. Terrestrial species are characterized by a body flattened from top to bottom (dorsoventrally). Ciliate (hairlike) scales on the margins of the eyelids or fringes on the toes indicate occurrence in sandy habitats. Some species are already full grown at 6 to 8 cm (2.5 to 3 in), but other agamids, such as the sailfins (*Hydrosaurus*), can reach the impressive total length of more than 1 meter (40 in).

Some agamids are spectacularly crested beauties of large size. This anglehead, *Gonocephalus grandis*, is one of the most heavily crested of the forest-dwelling agamids. Photo: U. Manthey.

Keeping and Breeding Agamids

FUNDAMENTAL CONSIDERATIONS

Agamids do not tolerate disturbance, particularly in the acclimation phase. Therefore, the terrarium must be completely finished before the lizards are introduced, including furnishings suitable for the special needs of the animals. Different temperature, moisture, and lighting regimes are indispensable for all agamids.

Sunlight, with its broad spectrum of electromagnetic radiation, controls the rhythm of life, the hormonal balance, and the metabolism and stimulates the immune system. Suitable for artificial lighting are lamps that produce a sunlike spectrum. For lighting the brighter sections of the terrarium, only halogen-vapor lamps (HQI, starting at 35 watts with a screw-in connector, at 70 watts with a plug and socket connection) equipped with reflectors are economically feasible. With smaller terraria, other halogen bulbs of 15 to 20 watts offer an alternative solution. For the darker region, full-spectrum fluorescent lamps have proved effective. They too should be housed in reflectors, so that all of the light shines in only one direction.

Sensibly arranged interior furnishings help to prevent constant visual contact between the terrarium inhabitants. They also offer a sufficient number of exposed sites for basking, hiding places, and shady spots. Suitable coverings of the back and sides make possible the optimal utilization of the terrarium. To achieve this, terrarium heights of at least 50 cm (20 in) are necessary, and 70 to 90 cm (28 to 36 in) would be ideal; higher cages make it harder to do maintenance on the back. The width is dependent on the size of the inhabitants and on how active they are, but should not be less than 70 cm (28 in) for smaller animals; medium-sized

Almost all agamids lay eggs, and most are happiest with a large land area. Females, like this *Agama aculeata*, may dig deep nests in which to lay the eggs. Photo: K. H. Switak.

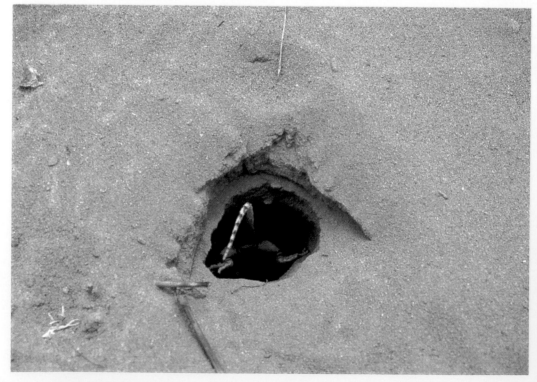

Gravid female agamids, especially of the genus *Agama* (like this *A. aculeata*), often assume distinctive color patterns that may be unique for each species. Photo: K. H. Switak.

agamids need 150 cm (5 ft) or more.

Adequate ventilation must be provided, the opening for getting rid of stagnant air always larger than the fresh-air opening.

TERRARIA FOR ARBOREAL AGAMIDS

No arboreal agamids limit their living space to only a single tree. Rather, they change their habitat within a certain territory. To feed or to defecate they often stay on the ground, and not infrequently their hiding places are also found there. Small, almost square terraria are therefore unsuitable for tree-dwellers. Tall and wide enclosures with large surface areas are much better suited to the behavior of the agamids.

A usable inside height of 60 to 70 cm (24 to 28 in) is adequate for only a few small arboreal agamids; for all other species 120 cm (4 ft) or more is necessary.

Two-thirds of the **dry-forest** terrarium is brightly lighted for 8 to 12 hours a day except during periods simulating the rainy season. Wire mesh (plastic is destroyed too quickly by the radiation and heat) separates the lamps from the rest of the terrarium. Between the warmest region (35 to 45°C, 95 to 115°F, directly under the light) and the coolest part of the terrarium, a temperature difference of about 15°C (25°F) should be strived for. Depending on the provenance of the species, a brief overwintering at lowered temperatures may be necessary. The simulation of dry and rainy periods often is advisable.

A wall with trickling water (covered with tree ferns or pebbles) falling into a small bowl produces the required humidity and simultaneously serves as a source of drinking water (standing water usually is not accepted). A small waterfall serves the same purpose. In this way the spraying of the interior furnishings with a misting bottle can be reduced to once or twice a week.

Rainforest terraria resemble the dry-forest terraria in size and furnishings. The humidity, however, reaches higher levels, and only a third is brightly lighted (a daily lighting period of 6 to 10 hours). Climatic changes are not necessary. Many begin-

Most agamids need to bask, and their requirements vary with their habitats. Your pet shop will have a variety of heat-emitting basking lights for you to choose from. Photo courtesy Coralife/Energy Savers.

Except for species that live deep in the rainforest shadows, all agamids need access to balanced full-spectrum lighting to mimic the sun. Special fluorescent full-spectrum lights are widely available. Photo courtesy Coralife/Energy Savers.

ners keep their rainforest agamids much too warm. The maximum temperature directly under the spotlight should be 35 to 38°C (95 to 100°F), and the temperature near the bottom should be only 20 to 25°C (68 to 77°F). A nocturnal cooling to 17 to 20°C (63 to 68°F) is essential. Supplemental heating generally is unnecessary because the heat given off by the lighting usually is adequate. The use of a forced ventilation system prevents the formation of undesirable fungi.

An aquatic section with a filter installed is obligatory, and a section for simulating rainfall or a fairly large waterfall, or both, for terraria wider than 1.5 meters (5 ft) also is necessary. A drain must be present to prevent the accumulation of water in the terrestrial section; in this connection a ceramic drain (such as is used in hydroculture) does a good job.

The **cloud-forest terrarium** is much the same as the rainforest terrarium. Characteristic of the cloud-forest terrarium are low temperatures with a large nocturnal drop in temperature. The highest temperature directly under the lamp is only between 30 and 35°C (86 and 95°F), the lowest near the bottom only 15 to 20°C (59 to 68°F). A nocturnal cooling to 12 to 17°C (54 to 63°F) should be attempted. The lamp with the greatest light intensity is only switched on four to six times a week.

Above: Heated rocks, which provide a lizard with heat from below, can be used as a supplement to a good basking light but should never be the the major source of heat in a terrarium. Photo courtesy Four Paws.
Below: Undertank heaters come in a variety of sizes and powers. They help provide a constant background terrarium temperature when the basking lights are turned off during the day. Photo courtesy Fluker Farms.

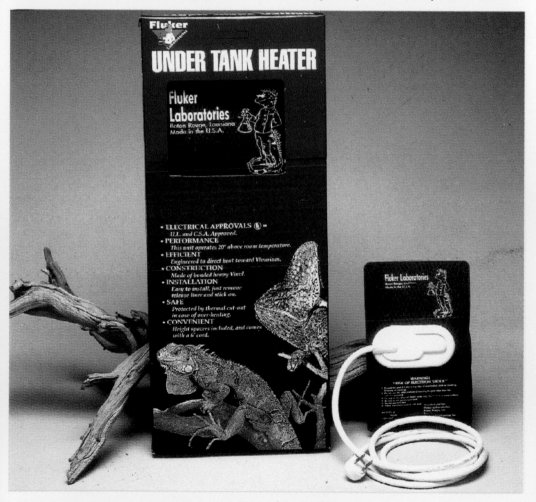

During the summer months, in particular, it should not be used as much or it will cause overheating.

TERRARIA FOR TERRESTRIAL AGAMIDS

Terrestrial agamids occur predominantly in arid or subarid zones characterized by intense sunshine. The term "terrestrial agamid" is not always appropriate, since many species are semi-arboreal (for example, *Agama agama* and *Laudakia atricollis*) or inhabit walls and rocks (for example, *Laudakia stellio* and *Agama atra*). In their habitats they use tree trunks, large rocks, bushes, and termite nests as lookout posts from which to watch for prey, rivals, and mates, as well as predators. Therefore, desert or arid terraria must not be too low. A height of 1 meter (40 in) or more has worked well. The terraria, with the exception of a few shady sites, must be as bright as possible. At the same time, however, excessive heat must be avoided.

A good substrate should be absorbent, non-toxic, and parasite-free. Litters made from treated plant material often are best for lizards. Photo courtesy Energy Savers.

Terrarium lining is a convenient, washable substrate for a few lizards kept in a display tank. Photo courtesy Four Paws.

In arid terraria rocky structures are the most natural kind of wall covering, but their weight is a serious problem. Suitable as a substitute are the stronger grades of styrofoam. With them all sorts of rocky structures can be reproduced almost true to nature. Several coats of epoxy resin containing a high percentage of kiln-dried quartz sand protect the soft material from the sharp claws of the agamids and give the artificial rock formations a natural look. (Caution: Epoxy resin is toxic while it cures; therefore, follow the application instructions exactly.)

The sand-filled bottom must be heated locally with a heating cable (various kinds are available in pet shops). For egg-laying it is important for the sand to be more than 15 cm (6 in) deep in a few places and that it is always kept slightly damp there. Because terrestrial agamids prefer to lay their eggs under rocks, the egg-laying sites can be covered with flat stones. They must be well anchored because some agamids like to undermine the stones. As a substitute, a piece of cork bark serves

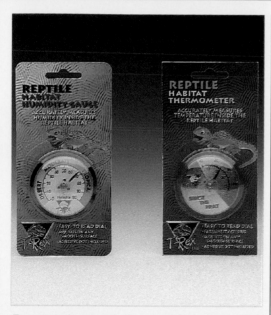

Every terrarium needs at least one thermometer that is easily readable. Recently small hygrometers (humidity meters) also have become available and make a useful addition to the terrarium furniture. Photo courtesy Ocean Nutrition.

All lizards need to be given a good reptile-grade calcium and vitamin supplement on a regular basis. Even adult lizards need supplements to maintain their active lifestyles. Photo courtesy American Reptile.

the same purpose. In the morning and especially in the evening, the rocks, back wall, and sand must be sprayed with clean water. As a result of the required nocturnal drop in temperature, a relative humidity of more than 90 percent is achieved. This percentage is attained even in deserts and leads to the formation of dew. Keeping conditions that are too dry or too wet are harmful. Daytime temperatures of 30 to 40°C (86 to 104°F) locally are essential for most terrestrial agamids.

Gnarled branches and roots are suitable as decoration. Particularly before and during the molt, some desert agamids like to bathe and defecate at the same time. A sufficiently large, but not too deep, dish kept constantly filled with fresh water completes the furnishings.

Literature: Abraham, 1983; Manthey, 1979, 1980a-d, 1981a-d, 1982, 1983; Matt, 1984.

DIET

Greatly simplified, we distinguish between herbivores and insectivores. Besides the true insects and their larvae, worms, spiders, and a few crustaceans often also are eaten. Small rodents and birds as well as other lizards also enrich the natural menu in some cases.

A broad variety of vitamins, supplements, and chemicals to make life easier for you and your pet is available at your local pet shop. Photo courtesy Energy Savers.

Prepared foods for iguanas are excellent for herbivorous agamids and also as supplements for those species that take mostly insects plus the occasional plant. Photo courtesy Ocean Nutrition.

Freeze-dried insects (mealworms, crickets, etc.) will be taken by many agamids once they get used to them. Photo courtesy Fluker Farms.

Prepared vegetable-based foods, such as these frozen iguana rations, will be taken by spiny-tailed agamids and other herbivorous species. Be sure all frozen foods are completely thawed before feeding. Photo courtesy Ocean Nutrition.

Meadows harbor a host of different small animals in the summer months. This "meadow plankton" is superbly suited for all agamids, which prefer live food. The winged stages of ants, which swarm out on their mating flight, are a special treat for small to medium-sized species. Some insects (for example, crickets, cockroaches, mealworms, migratory locusts, and wax moths) can be reared easily by the hobbyist or are available in pet shops.

The dietary palette of the herbivores likewise covers a broad spectrum. Many species eat with relish flower petals, the color of which plays a special role. Yellow and red flowers, in particular, are eaten downright ravenously. In the terrarium some specimens readily accept sweet fruit, whereas others prefer dandelion, kale, plantain, endive, lemon balm, rice, or various legumes.

Juveniles often need high-quality animal protein for optimal growth, which is why a high percentage of the diet consists of insects. With increasing age they are inclined to a predominantly herbivorous diet. This does not mean, however, that adult animals reject insects, but rather that they serve as a welcome supplemental food.

The substrate in your terrarium must match the requirements of your agamid. This female *Agama aculeata* might die of egg-binding if she were unable to dig a nest. Photo: K. H. Switak.

Food portions that are too large lead to a fatty liver condition. Terrestrial agamids therefore should be fed small portions at regular intervals.

It has been observed time and again that agamids change their taste in foods from day to day and suddenly refuse the foods that previously were eaten readily. Additionally, a one-sided diet leads to a variety of illnesses. Because the animals cannot be fed as varied a diet as they have in the wild, they are dependent on vitamin and calcium supplements to prevent deficiencies.

Literature: Friederich & Volland, 1981.

ACQUISITION

Experienced and adventurous hobbyists will want to go to appropriate vacation destinations to catch agamids there with their own hands, because knowledge of the original biotope is a valuable aid for keeping them later on. It should be kept in mind, however, that each hobbyist is obligated to obtain information on the regional and international conservation laws. Collecting may be illegal in some areas (Australia, for instance), and importations may be complicated or expensive. Obviously, few hobbyists will have the opportunity to travel to areas where agamids occur, so they are dependent on purchasing animals from the pet trade.

The purchase of captive-bred animals is recommended to all hobbyists. Poorly acclimated wild-caught specimens often present problems, and losses must be expected, so they are not really suitable for the average beginner to the terrarium hobby. (In agamids, a more attractive coloration than usual often indicates that they are at death's door.)

BREEDING AND REARING

A prerequisite for breeding is a healthy, compatible pair. Many agamids need particular climatic conditions before they begin courtship. While avoiding extreme values, seasonally dependent changes in climate must also be strived for in the terrarium. When the keeping conditions approach those found in the wild, the natural reproductive drive often is stimulated.

It is quite difficult to determine the proper dosage of vitamins and calcium required by the female during gestation. Weak youngsters or embryos that die in the egg could be the result of the incorrect diet of the mother.

Acclimated females instinctively lay their eggs in optimally damp places in the terrarium. The areas, of course, subsequently must never be permitted to dry out. When freshly hatched youngsters have dug themselves out of the soil, it can never be ruled out that other terrarium inhabitants will view them as food. A kitchen sieve placed over the laying site provides adequate protection. Many hobbyists carefully dig up the eggs and transfer them to an incubator without changing their orientation. They develop quite well at constant temperatures and high humidity in moist sand, foam rubber, or vermiculite. We do not recommend this method to beginners.

The requirements of young agamids with respect to their environment are similar to those of the adults, but they are more sensitive to too-high or too-low temperatures. In the first months of life, smaller terraria with temperature gradients and variable humidity have worked well because the food intake is easy to control there. Healthy young lizards have big appetites that often are accentuated by keeping them in groups. The size of the group depends on various factors and must be determined by careful observation in individual cases. Calcium supplements at about weekly intervals are absolutely necessary to prevent rachitis. With normal growth, the early transfer to larger terraria must be planned for. Juvenile agamids develop substantially better in large terraria than in small rearing enclosures.

ILLNESSES

The treatment of internal illnesses, which are often noticed far too late, can be carried out only by specially trained veterinarians. Most veterinarians are unqualified to treat these animals. Therefore, it is considerably more effective to prevent illness than to treat it. Appropriate care is the best insurance for healthy animals, though sometimes external injuries are unavoidable.

Many male agamids, such as this *Laudakia nupta fusca* from Africa, are more brightly colored than females and have larger spines or other specialized scales. Photo: R. D. Bartlett.

The prickle-nape *Acanthosaura armata* is typical of the group. Closely related to the angleheads, *Gonocephalus*, they have distinct raised "eyebrows." Photo: R. D. Bartlett.

Surveying the Agamids

The following section attempts to treat the genera and species of the agamids, of course with emphasis on the more often-seen species. The nomenclature is as modern as possible, but the hobbyist should remember that genera are constantly being reexamined by scientists to determine relationships and often are being split into smaller, more closely related groups of species. All the genera are treated in alphabetical order. As China and other Asian countries open their borders to exportation of lizards to the pet hobby, new species and even genera are entering the hobby all the time, and it is not impossible that species not included here will appear in the local pet shop on occasion.

Acanthosaura Gray, 1831

Prickle-napes: 4 species

Characteristics: Typical of the genus are more or less tall spines on the curve of the eyebrow and small, granulated dorsal scales that are interspersed with larger, tubercular scales. The body is laterally flattened. All species feature nape and dorsal crests as well as a visible tympanum. Prickle-napes can vary their coloration considerably. Males are distinguished from females by conspicuous, long hemipenis pouches.

Habits: These medium-sized arboreal agamids live in thick forests, usually near flowing water. Even species from the southern part of the range go through a yearly dormant period with reduced activity and food intake.

Keeping: Prickle-napes prefer a richly planted rainforest terrarium (H abt. 130, L abt. 100, D abt. 50 cm) with fairly thick vertical branches. These agamids prefer shaded sites, and flowing, filtered water seems to be essential for all species. After a brief acclimation period, their sedentary nature predominates if they do not happen to be hunting for food. In addition to insects they readily take earthworms; some eat fish and nestling mice.

Range: Burma, Thailand, western Malaysia, Indonesia (Anamba Islands), Cambodia, Laos, Vietnam, and southern China.

Acanthosaura armata (Hardwicke & Gray, 1827)

Description: HBL male, 115-140, female 110-120; TL male 160-165, female 140-150 mm; hatchlings 30 + 40 mm (HBL + TL). The long spines on the curve of the eyebrows and the occiput almost reach the height of the nape crest, which is composed of several closely spaced spines. They are either separated from the dorsal crest, which initially is the same height, by a gap of one or two crest scales or merge with it. Female and male possess a small throat pouch. In both sexes the dorsal side of the body is various shades of green to brown, allowing the lighter spots with dark margins to always stand out. The light ventral side can be greenish, brownish, or reddish.

Habitat and behavior: *Acanthosaura armata* prefers primary rainforests but also tolerates secondary forest. They perch motionless on trees and when danger threatens either do not move at all or move carefully to the side of the trunk away from the observer. If they are pursued further, they jump down like a flash and seek out shelter under tree roots or rocks.

Reproduction: Females are sexually mature at 18 months of age and a HBL of 100 mm. The eggs are laid four months after copulation. A clutch contains 12 to 15 eggs (average size 11 x 19.5 mm), but that of a young female may have only nine. The female takes several days to find the most suitable laying site by making test

Acanthosaura crucigera. Photo: R. G. Sprackland.

cxcavations. During the very long incubation period of 191 to 193 days, the eggs grow to about 20 x 27.5 mm at 21 to 25°C (70 to 77°F). Egg retention (amphigonia retardata) has been documented.

Notes: The breeding group can consist of only one male and one female, because weaker conspecifics are suppressed. *Acanthosaura armata* does well when kept with *Acanthosaura crucigera*, *Gonocephalus* species (except for *Gonocephalus grandis*), and amphibians from the same area of occurrence. Because the agamids are highly voracious, the food intake of other terrarium inhabitants must be controlled. The same is true of juvenile prickle-napes, of which groups of no more than four or five animals of the same size can be reared successfully. From previous experience, certain wild-caught animals at first eat earthworms almost exclusively.

Range: Altitudes of 0-750 meters, Thai/Malaysian Peninsula (northernmost province of Nakhon Si Thammarat), Pinang and Tioman Islands, as well as the Indonesian Anamba Islands.

Literature: Steiof et al., 1991.

Above: Taxonomy of the prickle-napes is difficult at best. *Acanthosaura armata*, shown here, closely resembles *A. crucigera* but lacks the gular pouch. Photo: R. D. Bartlett.

Top right: Habitat of *Acanthosaura armata* in the primary rainforest. Photo: U. Manthey.

Right: A female *Acanthosaura armata* from the Tioman Islands off the Malaysian Peninsula. Photo: U. Manthey.

Acanthosaura capra Guenther, 1861

Description: HBL 130, TL 175 mm. *Acanthosaura capra* is the only species of the genus lacking spines on the occiput. Males possess a very large throat pouch, the yellowish ground color of which is decorated with green streaking. The tall nape crest is clearly separated from the somewhat lower dorsal crest. Both consist of lanceolate scales, the bases of which are broader than in other prickle-napes. The olive back covers a brown network. On the yellowish head of males a broad green band extends from the outer eye ring to the shoulder. A stripe of the same color is present on the nape alongside the crest. The eye is surrounded by a light green ring that encloses a wider dark green one.

Habitat and behavior: As far as is known, this agamid lives in the tops of large rainforest trees.

Notes: *Acanthosaura capra* sometimes eats smaller lizards.

Range: Cambodia, Laos, Vietnam.

Acanthosaura crucigera Boulenger, 1885

Description: HBL male, 97-100, female 90-97; TL male 162, female 122-140 mm. Spines are present on the nape and occiput; the dorsal crest is clearly set off from the taller nape crest by a wide gap. The crest scales are spiny or triangular, with the tips pointing upward, not touching at the base, usually separated by a gap of one scale. This species is extremely variable in coloration, often with a dark network with lighter spots; the sides of the head to under the eyes as well as a rhomboid patch on the nape are always dark brown to black.

Habitat and behavior: Found in rainforests and montane forests to 1800 meters. Though it lives in trees, it seeks out hiding places on the ground.

Reproduction: This prickle-nape lays 10 to 12 eggs (12 x 20 mm).

Range: Burma, Thailand, northern Malaysian Peninsula, Cambodia, southern Vietnam.

Though the spine over the eye is variable in length in many prickle-napes, it usually is present. This seems to be a male *Acanthosaura crucigera* because of the eye-patch. Photo: A. Norman.

A gorgeous male *Acanthosaura crucigera* displaying an expanded gular pouch typical of the species. Notice the large spine over the eye and the other one over the tympanum. Photo: K. Nemuras.

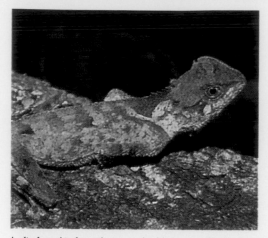

Left: A male *Acanthosaura lepidogaster*. Right: A male *Acanthosaura crucigera*. Photos: Left: Vogel; Right: U. Manthey.

Acanthosaura lepidogaster Cuvier, 1829

Description: HBL male 72-111, female 85-107; TL male 118-165, female 110-157 mm. Spines on the curve of the eyebrows and occiput are short. The dorsal crest is interrupted in the nape region or continuous, with very short, closely spaced, triangular scales with tips pointing to the rear. Coloration variable, male and female often brownish, but males often with a white throat and margins of the lips yellow; top of head, a large triangle on each side of the head, and a rhomboidal patch in the nape region are black; a fold of skin on shoulder likewise is black, edged in white. There are light patches with dark borders on the back, and the sides are marbled in green and black. Other combinations of colors are possible, and females also turn green.

Habitat and behavior: Montane forests, about 700-900 meters, often on the ground. Provide a mild hibernation lasting one or two months.

Range: Burma, northern Thailand, Cambodia, Laos, Vietnam, southern China, and the island of Hainan.

Literature: Mell, 1952.

Agama Daudin, 1802

Agamas: approximately 27-35 species and some 20-25 subspecies

Characteristics: The heavy body and triangular head are weakly flattened dorsoventrally. The head has a large, round tympanum and a throat (gular) fold, but no gular pouch. Many species possess a short nape crest. The tail is covered with shingle-like scales. Preanal pores are exhibited only by males, which usually surpass the females in size and attractive coloration.

Habits: *Agama* species inhabit savannahs, arid forests, and desertlike regions with sparse vegetation. Some have become followers of civilization. Animals from desertlike regions usually lead solitary lives, but predominantly arboreal agamids display a stable social structure. In these groups a male can be dominant over several females and juveniles. The rather shy agamids often feed on smaller lizards, flowers, and fruits in addition to insects.

Distribution of the genus *Agama* in the restricted sense.

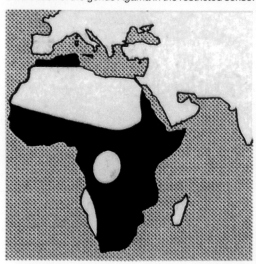

Keeping: For arboreal and rock-dwelling species, provide a dry-forest terrarium (H abt. 150, L abt. 150, D abt. 80 cm). The bottom is filled with coarse sand and is decorated with a few rocks. For terrestrial species, an arid terrarium (H abt. 100, L abt. 180, D abt. 80 cm) with the same substrate is suitable.

Range: Africa except for the Namib and Sahara deserts and the Congo Basin.

blue colors. Particularly with pregnant females, orange lateral spots and turquoise dots stand out on the head.

Habitat and behavior: *Agama agama lionotus* lives on trees and on the ground, but as a follower of civilization it also can be found on houses, walls, and in dumps. An alpha male can command a "harem" of up to 25 females and half-grown animals. Moreover, a dominant female often does

A dominant male House Agama, *Agama agama lionotus*, displays a contrasting orange head and blue body and tail. Photo: Grossmann.

Agama agama (Linnaeus, 1758)

Agama agama lionotus Boulenger, 1896

House Agama

Description: HBL male 107-137, female 84-120; TL male 210-263, female 164-198 mm; hatchlings 55-60 mm TL. Only males possess a low nape crest. The gray-brown back often is covered with a pattern of dark patches. With sufficient warmth, the head, throat, and shoulders of dominant males turn orange red, the body and the extremities dark blue. The cross-banded tail exhibits pale and dark

not leave the dominant male's side to fend off other female courtiers.

Reproduction: After the start of the rainy season, females lay three to eight eggs in self-excavated holes or in deep, damp tree cracks. The youngsters hatch two to three months later.

Notes: Based on our experience, only one pair of adults may be kept with the youngsters.

Range: *Agama agama agama*—central Africa; *Agama agama africana*—Liberia; *Agama agama boensis*—Guinea-Bissau; *Agama agama dodomae*—Tanzania; *Agama agama elgonis*—Uganda, Kenya,

A female *Agama aculeata* disappearing into the nest in which she will lay her eggs. Notice that the tail scales are not in regular whorls under the tail. Photo: K. H. Switak.

Agama aculeata is the Ground Agama of most of southern Africa's dry savannas. Males develop bright blue on the sides of the head when ready to breed. Photo: K. H. Switak.

A female Ground Agama, *Agama aculeata*, laying her eggs. Color patterns of agamas vary greatly with sex, age, and behavior. Photo: K. H. Switak.

Males of two agamas from Namibia, formerly South-western Africa. These are species of rocky, dry deserts subject to tremendous temperature changes. Above: A Southern Rock Agama, *Agama atra knobeli*, from southern Namibia. Photo: P. Freed. Below: A Namibian Rock Agama, *Agama planiceps*, from northern Namibia. Photo: J. Visser.

Many African agamas have rather small ranges. The Somali Rock Agama, *Agama persimilis*, is found mostly in Somalia and adjacent areas of Ethiopia. Males develop a gorgeous blue undersurface, while females (inset) are plain. Photos: P. Freed.

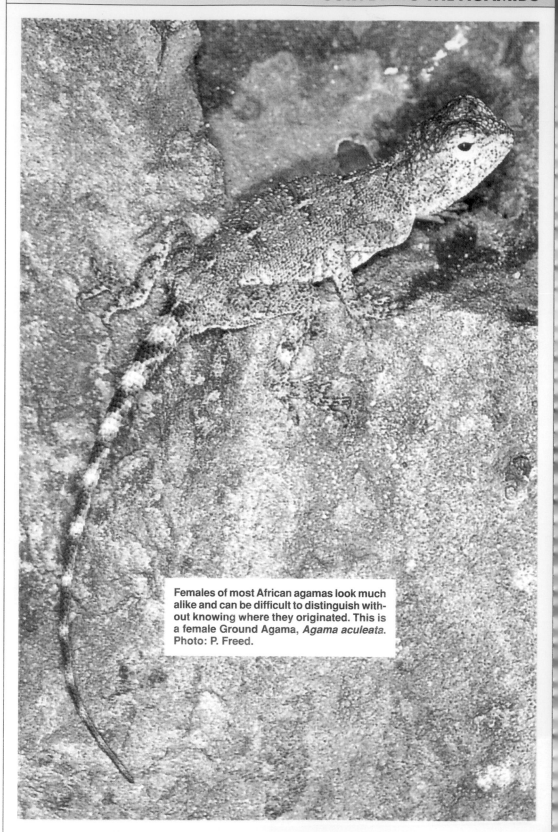

Females of most African agamas look much alike and can be difficult to distinguish without knowing where they originated. This is a female Ground Agama, *Agama aculeata*. Photo: P. Freed.

Tanzania; *Agama agama lionotus*—Uganda, Kenya; *Agama agama mucosoensis*—Angola; *Agama agama savattieri*—central Africa; *Agama agama spinosa*—Egypt to Ethiopia; *Agama agama ufipae*—Lake Tanganyika (from Wermuth, 1967).

Amphibolurus Wagler, 1830

Jacky Dragons: 8 species, 2 subspecies

Characteristics: The medium-sized *Amphibolurus* species exhibit slender, laterally flattened bodies with elongated heads and long tails. The tympanum is always visible, and femoral and preanal pores are present. Almost all species have medium-height, erectile nape crests and low dorsal crests that are better developed in males. Further typical characters of the males are the conspicuous hemipenis pouches and the ability to turn the throat black in color. The rather plain body colors often are broken by light dorsolateral and lip stripes. As used here, the genus includes several species often assigned to the genus *Lophognathus* in Australian literature.

Habits: These generally terrestrial agamids prefer the margins of flowing bodies of water in open shrubby and forested landscapes. Males in particular often perch in exposed places and survey their territory. They find hiding places under large rocks, tree stumps, or crevices. Their diet consists of insects and small lizards. They estivate during the dry season.

Keeping: In an arid-forest terrarium (H abt. 120, W abt. 120, D abt. 80 cm) with a sandy bottom, plants, and rock formations, these agamids do well when kept in pairs. They soon lose their shyness and take food from the hand.

Range: Australia and southern New Guinea.

Amphibolurus longirostris (Boulenger, 1883)

Description: HBL male 114; TL 356 mm, female somewhat smaller. The dorsal crest is tallest in the nape region. The gray to reddish brown back displays a faint pattern of spots or sometimes reddish brown

Agama aculeata armata is the subspecies of the Ground Agama that occurs from Zimbabwe to Tanzania and south into Natal and the Transkei. The several subspecies of this species differ in keeling of the head and belly scales. Photo: K. H. Switak.

cross-bands. Broad, conspicuous white longitudinal stripes mark the lips and the dorsolateral region and can be connected by a thin white line over the snout. Above the lips the head of the male is bright reddish. In contrast, an oval black patch is located over the tympanum.

Habitat and behavior: These agamids are found most frequently in deep gorges with flowing water or ponds. They live there in mangroves or far from water on steep red cliffs. In cool weather the lizards hide in caves and holes, and on warm days they sleep on branches and twigs.

Reproduction: After fairly long periods of rainfall, females lay three to six eggs up to twice a year.

Range: Western and central Australia.

Aphaniotis Peters, 1864

Blue-mouthed Agamas: 4 species

Characteristics: Typical of the genus are the more or less distinct frontal appendages in the form of tuberculate or conical scales, concealed or at most tiny tympana, a nonhomogeneous (i.e., scales of mixed types) dorsal scaling, and weakly developed nape and dorsal crests. The body is laterally flattened.

Habits: These delicate tree- and shrub-dwellers live in rainforests near flowing water.

Keeping: Provide a planted rainforest terrarium or cloud-forest terrarium for the highland species and equip it with fairly thin vertical and diagonal branches (H abt. 90, L abt. 70, D abt. 50 cm). The blue-mouths of the lowlands do well in the terrarium, where they feed on small insects.

Range: Altitudes of 0-1800 meters, Thai/Malaysian Peninsula, Borneo, Sumatra, and on numerous surrounding islands.

Aphaniotis acutirostris Modigliani, 1889

Description: HBL male 46-60, female 45-54; TL male 96-127, female 90-106 mm. Very small granular and roof-tilelike scales of different sizes cover the back. Parallel to the middorsal line there is a row of tubercular scales on both sides. A tubercular, elongated scale, which is larger in males, is located on the tip of the snout. The nape crest is only very weakly expressed; males can, however, erect a small nape crest. In addition, males have a

The species now in the genus *Amphibolurus* bear little resemblance to the bearded dragons, now in *Pogona*, that once resided here. This is *Amphibolurus longirostris* from central and western Australia. Photo: Eidenmueller.

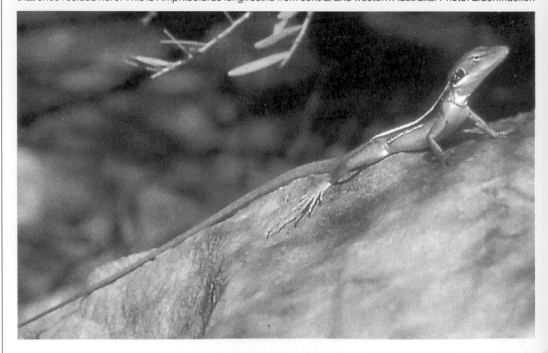

Two species of Australian jacky dragons. Above: *Amphibolurus nobbi*, the Nobbi Dragon, occurs in dry habitats over much of eastern Australia. Photo: S. Minton. Below: The Common Jacky Dragon, *A. muricatus*, is somewhat more southeastern in distribution. Photo: J. Coborn.

conspicuous yellow throat pouch, but they seldom display it. There is only the suggestion of a brownish throat disk in females. In both sexes, lighter and darker markings or patterns break up the brownish ground color. The yellowish to green vertical bands of the male form an attractive contrast to the ground color. Females sometimes exhibit pale brown vertical bands. They also occasionally display a pale brown longitudinal band, with a dark or light border, extending across the back. The inside of the mouth is blue.

Habitat and behavior: In the lowland rainforests of northern Sumatra, these small agamids not infrequently are found on bushy smaller trees and on the ground.

Reproduction: Normally these agamids lay two eggs (7 x 12 mm) at intervals of 30 to 100 days. These require an incubation period of 48 to 63 days at an average temperature of 26 to 29°C (79 to 84°F).

Range: Sumatra and the islands to the west, possibly Borneo.

A male *Aphaniotis acutirostris* from northern Sumatra. Photo: U. Manthey.

Aphaniotis fusca Peters, 1864

Description: HBL male 61-67, female 52-61; TL male 141- 156, female 112-144 mm; hatchlings 23-43 mm (HBL + TL). Short triangular scales form the suggestion of a nape crest, which does not extend onto the back. Small dorsal scales are mixed with larger ones. A frontal appendage is barely visible. Females possess a somewhat smaller gular pouch than do males. Both sexes exhibit a brownish or light olive to green back with scattered, indistinct brown spots or vertical bands in places. Juveniles exhibit dark brown flanks and light dorsal markings. The iris is a gleaming blue (adult males) or brown (females and juveniles). The inside of the mouth is blue.

A female *Aphaniotis fusca* from the Tioman Islands. Photo: U. Manthey.

Habitat and behavior: Whole families perch quite close together on thin tree trunks of the shady lowland rainforest.

Reproduction: The female lays one or two eggs (7 x 18 mm) at relatively short intervals. They develop well in moist soil at 20 to 22°C (68 to 72°F).

Notes: Females and juveniles, in particular, need a lot of calcium. If the diet is deficient in calcium, the juveniles die at the latest after half a year, although they feed without problems.

Range: Thai/Malaysian Peninsula, Pulau Tioman; Sumatra and surrounding islands?; Natuna Islands; Borneo.

Brachysaura Blyth, 1856

Night Agamas: 1 species

Characteristics: The body is slightly flattened laterally. All dorsal scales are of uniform size, shingle-like, and regularly arranged. The tail length is equal to or somewhat less than the head-body length (HBL).

Habits: This genus contains what seems to be the only species of agamid whose active period falls in the crepuscular (dawn and dusk) and nocturnal hours. As ground-dwellers they use preexisting holes in the ground as hiding places. Their movements seem ponderous, and often they make no attempt to escape when approached.

Keeping: *Brachysaura* is an easy-to-keep, undemanding charge. Arid terraria with a deep substrate (a mixture of loam and sand) and pre-excavated holes are suitable for keeping these agamids. The lighting should be controlled so a crepuscular period is produced; a blue lamp simulates moonlight at night. In this way it is possible to observe the nocturnal doings of these insectivores without obtrusive light from a flashlight.

Range: Southeastern Pakistan to the Ganges valley, India.

Brachysaura minor (Hardwicke & Gray, 1827)

Description: HBL male 85-90; TL up to 90 mm, female larger. A tiny crest of triangular scales extends from the occiput to the tail. Two separate spines, which can be surrounded by smaller ones, extend above the tympanum. The keeled dorsal scales are pointed upward and toward the rear. Males possess a thickened base of the tail. The back is olive and displays three rows of dark spots with light borders, the middle row the most conspicuous. On each side of the nape is a light stripe forked to the rear, and a light vertical band extends from the eye to the mouth. Unlike the case in most agamid genera, females are distinguished by a more brilliant coloration. In breeding condition they exhibit a rich red except for the olive back and the deep-black throat fold. Juveniles display dark dorsal spots with bright red borders on a reddish brown background.

Literature: Smith, 1935.

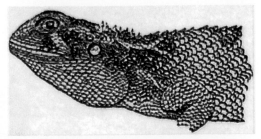

Many agamids are virtually unknown. This represents *Brachysaura minor*.

Bronchocela Kaup, 1827

Slender Agamas: 7 species

Characteristics: *Bronchocela* species have a slender, laterally flattened body with an extremely long tail (three or four times the HBL). They attain a maximum head-body length (HBL) of 150-160 mm. In comparison to the closely related *Calotes* species, their heads and legs are longer and their dorsal scales smaller. Spiny or conical scales are absent on the occiput and curve of the eyebrow. The individual species are difficult to distinguish, as are the sexes.

Habits: These attractively colored agamids prefer bright, warm locales outside of dense forests and often are followers of civilization.

Keeping: Depending on the provenance of the animals, they need a planted dry-forest, rainforest, or cloud-forest terrarium with intense lighting (H abt. 120, L abt. 150, D abt. 60 cm) and both thick and thin branches. The agamids are rather restless in the terrarium. Based on the little available experience, they must be considered as delicate and short-lived. During the warm summer months it should be possible to keep them in the outdoor terrarium or greenhouse. They are insectivores that apparently do not pass up small lizards either.

Range: Altitudes of 0-1600 meters, Burma to Vietnam, Nicobar Islands, Philippines, Thai/Malaysian Peninsula, Indo-Australasian Archipelago (east to New Guinea).

Bronchocela cristatella (Kuhl, 1820)

Characteristics: HBL male 87-110, female 82-96; TL male 300-350, female 290-330 mm; in some populations the HBL can be up to 130, the TL up to 440 milli-meters. A small nape crest of lanceolate scales is present, and there is a sugges-tion of a dorsal crest consisting of low, serrated scales. A small gular pouch is present. Usually these lizards are green with light spots that can form vertical bars on the sides; rapid changes in color to yellow, brown, or black are possible. The throat pouch of males sometimes is red-dish, while the head is whitish with a blue band.

Though they resemble *Calotes*, slender agamas, such as this male *Bronchocela cristatella*, are much more slender and have smaller scales. Photo: U. Manthey.

Habitat and reproduction: One to two spindle-shaped eggs (9 x 42 mm) are laid. The lizards are found in trees and bushes on forest edges and also are a follower of civilization.

Range: Altitudes of 0-1600 meters, Burma to New Guinea and Philippines.

Bronchocela jubata Dumeril & Bibron, 1837

Characteristics: HBL 130-150, TL 440-450 mm; hatchlings 145-162 mm. The nape and dorsal crest are made of lan-ceolate scales pointing back. The gular pouch reaches to the chest. The body color generally is green, with rapid changes in color to brown or black. There may be yellow or red spots or vertical bars.

Habitat and behavior: These aggres-sive lizards are found in trees and hedges and also are followers of civilization.

Reproduction: Two spindle-shaped eggs (9.5-12 x 40-53 mm) are laid and hatch in 84 days.

Range: Java and nearby islands; Bali; possibly Nicobar Islands and Sulawesi.

Literature: Kopstein, 1938.

Caimanops Storr, 1974

Five-keel Agamas: 1 species

Characteristics: The most obvious fea-ture of the genus is the presence of five longitudinal rows of fairly large, keeled scales on the back of the laterally flat-tened body. The legs are thin, the tail short. There is a visible tympanum, but there are no femoral pores.

Habits and behavior: This semi-arbo-real and terrestrial species specializes is feeding on termites and prefers regions with red soils and acacias. They often are found under fallen trees. When danger threatens they depend on their camou-flage and perch motionless.

Notes: The single species, *C. amphiboluroides* (Lucas & Frost, 1902) has a HBL to 94 mm, TL 160 mm. On the pale green, greenish brown, or pale brown flanks are dark stripes of variable width that continue onto the belly. There also is a pattern of dark spots on the head. The species lays eggs. For keeping this spe-cies, a dry-forest terrarium (H abt. 100, W abt. 120, D abt. 80 cm) with a sandy substrate and branched climbing branches is suitable.

Range: Central Western Australia.

Calotes Cuvier, 1817

Beauty Lizards, Bloodsuckers: 16-20 species, 2 subspecies

Characteristics: All species have a laterally flattened body with shingle-like, regularly arranged dorsal scales of nearly uniform size. Spines or conical scales usually are present on the occiput, on the curve of the eyebrow, or both; the tympanum is visible. A thicker base of the tail as well as taller nape and dorsal crests are characteristic of males; the dorsal crest occasionally is absent in females. The smallest species attain a head-body length (HBL) of 70 mm, the largest 145 mm. Their extraordinarily variable coloration makes any description seem incomplete.

To simplify identification, the *Calotes* species are divided into two groups:

I) *Calotes liocephalus* group. The lateral scales point backward but not upward near the base of the tail. Species: *andamanensis, ceylonensis, elliotti, liocephalus, liolepis, nigrilabris, rouxi.*

II) *Calotes versicolor* group. The lateral scales point backward and upward near the base of the tail. Species: *bhutanensis, calotes, emma, grandisquamis, jerdoni, maria, mystaceus, nemoricola, versicolor.*

Not included in either group are: *kinabaluensis, kingdonwardi, medogensis,* and *nigrigularis,* because it seems questionable whether they even belong to the genus.

Habits: Beauty lizards prefer open landscapes or light, sun-drenched forests. They are often encountered on fence posts, boulders, slopes, and on the ground. Several species, often called garden lizards, are followers of civilization. The pugnacity of the males as well as their strong tendency to territory formation are well known.

Keeping: A lightly planted dry-forest terrarium (H abt. 130, W abt. 180, D abt. 70 cm) with a few branches and rocks will suffice. *Calotes* species often are lizard-eaters, although their diet consists mainly of insects.

Range: Altitudes of 0-2100 meters, Iran to southern China, north to the Himalayas, south to the Maldive Islands and Sri Lanka as well as Sumatra.

Calotes calotes (Linnaeus, 1758)
Common Beauty Lizard, Green Blood-sucker

Description: HBL male 90-130; TL male 400-500; female somewhat smaller. The highest point of the sawlike dorsal-crest scales is in the nape region, the crest becoming considerably lower toward the tail. Males possess distinctly longer crest scales than do females. Above the tympanum is a row of spines of varying heights. On a generally bright green (but some-

When *Bronchocela cristatella* appears in the hobby, it usually is listed as a species of *Calotes*. Photo: R. D. Bartlett.

times brown or almost black) back there are four to seven whitish or dark vertical stripes. Females also can be marked with a whitish dorsolateral longitudinal stripe. The head color of the male varies from dark red through orange (leading to the name Bloodsucker) to light green. In addition, there are white to blackish blue patches above the tympanum and eye.

Habitat and behavior: On Sri Lanka, *Calotes calotes* is more commonly found in the moist montane zones to a maximum altitude of 1500 meters than in the dry plains. Small trees, bushes, and thickly grown slopes near flowing water are favorite habitats of this excellent swimmer.

Reproduction: The timing of reproduction in the moist zones of Sri Lanka is seasonally dependent, and in the dry regions of the island breeding is limited to the rainy season. Clutches consist of 6 to 12 eggs (12 x 18 mm). The at first predominantly brownish young hatch after an incubation period of 79 to 84 days at 20 to 26°C (68 to 79°F).

Notes: Wild-caught specimens are very nervous during the acclimation phase and often refuse food insects. Smaller lizards (for example, deformed geckos) are clearly the preferred food and apparently contribute to successful keeping. Constantly aggressive males often put females into stressful situations that are signaled by a dark brown coloration. In such cases the sexes must be separated for a time. Youngsters and pregnant females need high doses of calcium and vitamins. *Calotes calotes* is delicate and does not survive much longer than two years in the terrarium.

Range: Sri Lanka, southwestern India (Travancore, Shevaroy Hills), and the Nicobar Islands.

Calotes emma emma Gray, 1845
White-banded Beauty Lizard

Description: HBL male 105-115; TL male up to 290 mm; female somewhat smaller; hatchlings 32 + 90 mm (HBL + TL). The dorsal crest consists of tall lanceolate nape and serrate dorsal scales that become considerably lower toward the tail. The dorsal crest of the female is made up of very short serrate scales. At the caudal end of the curve of the eyebrow

and above the tympanum there are spiny scales of varying heights surrounded by smaller ones.

In territorial males in full color, a conspicuous red tone may adorn the front part of the back, the top of the head, and a broad stripe from the tip of the snout to the occiput, while a flat black triangle provides a contrasting head adornment. The throat, gular pouch, and front legs as well as the front half of the sides of the body are likewise more or less black, in part with light speckling. From the occiput to the tail extends an almost white dorsolateral stripe. The entire reddish brown rear half of the body is overlain with dark rhomboidal markings on the back and frequently also on the flanks. Females have a yellow gular pouch with black spots or stripes. The head, front of the body, and front legs are rich reddish orange to rust red. There is a conspicuous black shoulder stripe. The rear half of the body, including the extremities, is pale reddish brown with indistinct dark vertical bars across the back. This coloration was exhibited by *Calotes emma emma* from the Khao Yai National Park (650 meters above sea level) during the dry season in May. During the rainy season in August, male specimens from southern Thailand exhibit, besides a reddish black coloration, mostly shades of green broken up by variable brownish or black markings. In March the whole front part of the body including the head, throat, and extremities can be blue, with the exception of a black shoulder stripe and the black rear half of the body. Only the dorsolateral stripe, which is always light, is not affected by changes in color.

Habitat and behavior: *Calotes emma emma* seems to be more closely bound to forests than are other *Calotes* species. They prefer sun-drenched locations on forest edges, such as along broader bodies of water. This habitat also suits *Calotes versicolor* in southern Thailand, so both species can found not far apart from each other. They principally perch on tree trunks or thin branches. The juveniles initially grow up together on the ground. *Calotes emma emma* is one of the agamids capable of producing vocalizations. When they are

Calotes species are very average agamids, and in some ways they could be thought of as the Old World equivalents of the American anoles. They are aggressive, often change colors, and often do well in the presence of man.

captured and held they make distinct squeaking sounds.

Reproduction: Females from southern Thailand laid four to six eggs (maximum of 12 eggs, 11 x 17 millimeters) in August. At an average temperature of 25 to 28°C (77 to 82°F) the youngsters hatched after 62 to 74 days, but after 100 days at an average of 19 to 22°C (66 to 72°F).

Notes: Animals from the southern part of the range need rainforest terraria, but dry-forest terraria with simulated rainy and dry seasons are necessary for the northern population. A precise knowledge of the collecting site is therefore essential for appropriate care.

Range: *Calotes emma emma*—Assam, India; Burma, Thailand, northern Malaysian Peninsula, Cambodia, Laos, Vietnam; *Calotes emma alticristatus*—northern Thailand, southern China (Yunnan).

Calotes mystaceus Dumeril & Bibron, 1837

Turquoise Garden Lizard

Description: The size apparently varies geographically: HBL male 95, female 85; TL male 200, female 173 mm; or HBL male 140, TL 280 mm, female somewhat smaller; hatchlings 24-26 + 40-46 mm (HBL + TL). Two spiny scales, which may be surrounded by smaller ones, are present on each side of the occiput. The continuous nape and dorsal crest of the male is composed of short, triangular scales in the rear quarter of the body. The dorsal crest of the female extends only to about the middle of the body. The bright blue to turquoise coloration of the front part of the body in the male, including the head and front legs, makes for a fascinating display. Shades of dark blue to violet set off the throat and gular pouch. A broad whitish or yellow stripe extends under the eye from the tip of the snout to the shoulder. Each side of the back is adorned by four large reddish to brown patches, but the entire back can also appear brownish or grayish, in which case the light stripes on the head and the dark dorsal patches are retained, but the throat region then looks reddish. Females display a similar, but not as bright, coloration. Newly hatched youngsters are uniformly gray with dark crossbars.

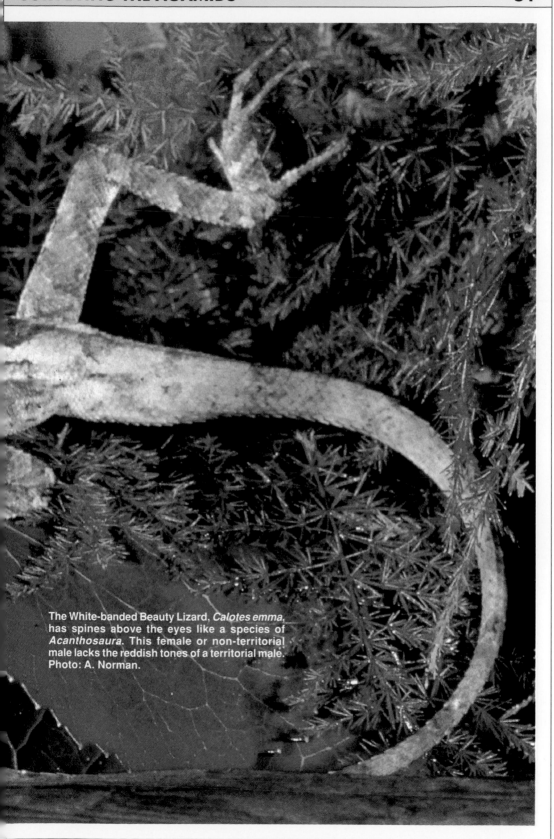

The White-banded Beauty Lizard, *Calotes emma*, has spines above the eyes like a species of *Acanthosaura*. This female or non-territorial male lacks the reddish tones of a territorial male. Photo: A. Norman.

The Turquoise Garden Lizard, *Calotes mystaceus*, is a common city lizard in much of Thailand. Occasional specimens are imported for the terrarium hobby, but their subtle colors seldom draw much attention. Photos: W. Wuster.

Habitat and behavior: *Calotes mystaceus* is a follower of civilization that can be found even in the middle of Bangkok on trees. Outside of the cities it is found on trees along roads and in light forests. The display coloration of males also is exhibited when a potential predator is spotted.

Reproduction: During the dry season in about February to March the males begin courting in their brightest colors. The breeding season extends from April to May. During the monsoon season in June, 7 to 11 eggs (10-11 x 15-18 mm) are laid. At an average temperature of 24 to 26°C (75 to 79°F), the youngsters hatch after 60 to 70 days.

Range: Altitudes of 0-1500 meters, Burma, Thailand, Laos, Cambodia, Vietnam, Andaman and Nicobar Islands.

***Calotes versicolor* (Daudin, 1802)**
Brown Garden Lizard
Description: HBL male 90-140, female 65-120; TL male 270-350, female 155-240 mm; hatchlings 21-27 + 32-53 (HBL + TL). The size varies geographically, the largest specimens coming from the plains of the western part of the range. Above the tympanum on both sides of the head are located two spines or a group of spines. Males have a continuous dorsal crest from the nape to the base of the tail. In females it covers at most the first third of the back, often only the nape. These secondary sex differences can be recognized in certain populations immediately after hatching, but in others only at an age of five to six months. At this age the males begin to exhibit the first clear changes in color. Females and especially males display extraordinary variation in their coloration and markings. As a rule, juveniles and females from Sri Lanka display a light or dark dorsolateral stripe on each side of the back extending from the eye to the tail. Often the back also is adorned with light

A beautiful male *Calotes*, possibly related to *C. versicolor*. Identification of garden lizards is difficult even if you know where they originated. Often these lizards are imported as females and young in small numbers. Photo: P. Freed.

The colorful red head of *Calotes calotes* has led to the common name "Bloodsucker" for these lizards. Photo: U. Manthey.

In full color, the male *Calotes mystaceus* truly deserves the name Turquoise Garden Lizard. Expect a lot of variation from specimen to specimen. This specimen came from Pak Chong, Thailand. Photo: U. Manthey.

Though this garden lizard often is imported as *Calotes versicolor*, it appears to be a quite different species. Regardless of its name, this is a very pretty male. Photo: R. D. Bartlett.

or dark vertical bands. The markings of the males can be similar, but look washed out in old specimens. In displaying males there usually are no markings visible at all. The head turns a bright yellow, the gular pouch is resplendent with a rich brick red, yellow or red dominates on the body, and the extremities are a contrasting black. Males from southern Thailand exhibit red heads and gular pouches and yellow bodies and extremities. A black shoulder stripe and black cheeks also stand out.

Habitat and behavior: *Calotes versicolor* is considered to be purely a follower of civilization that is not bound to any particular biotope. It colonizes open landscapes with bushes and scattered trees as well as rocky regions. It is found just as commonly on the ground as on trees. Deforestation and road construction are making it possible for this lizard to extend its range. For example, they now are found at altitudes where they were not present formerly. At the same time they suppress or wipe out smaller species of agamids by eating the young. Populations from the northern parts of the range undergo a kind of hibernation during which activity and food intake are sharply restricted.

Reproduction: The breeding season begins just before the rainy season and is ushered in by the change in color and territorial fights of the males. From exposed places they survey their surroundings, nod with the head and front of the body, and spread their gular pouch in a threat posture. In this way they challenge other males. Two males preparing to fight first watch each other from a distance, approach in a straight line, and go at each other. In so doing both stand on their hind legs and tail, grasp each other with the front legs, and try to bite the opponent. If neither decides to retreat, not infrequently serious injuries occur. Once the territories have been divided, the females are courted. Copulations last only a few seconds, but are performed several times at 20-minute intervals. In the middle of the rainy season the females lay 1 to 25 eggs

Notice the weakly distinguished black spot above the base of the front leg in this male *Calotes* species, often misidentified as *C. versicolor*. If visible, this is a good indicator for the species, whatever its proper name. Photo: P. Freed.

(4-13 x 10-19 mm). Depending on temperature, the young hatch after 37 to 79 days (the latter value for 22 to 23°C, 72 to 73°F). Just before hatching the eggs will have reached a size of 10-15 x 14-23 mm. *Calotes versicolor* reaches sexual maturity at 9 to 12 months.

Notes: Wild-caught specimens and females during the breeding season often strike against the terrarium panes with the snout. The glass should be prepared so that they cannot see their reflection. A breeding pair must come from the same region, because the testes and ovaries grow in a particular yearly rhythm and then degenerate again. Rearing enclosures with dimensions of 70 x 60 x 60 cm (H x L x D) furnished with bushy plants have

Male-male agonistic behavior in *Calotes versicolor*. Photos: U. Manthey.

This unidentified *Calotes* shows a tinge of red on the lips, the origin of the folk legend that it literally "sucks blood." Photo: Chen Keng Loon.

worked well in the first seven months of life. Caution is advised, because even juveniles will feed on smaller lizards.

Range: Altitudes of 0-2100 meters, Iran to southern China, south to the Maldives and Sumatra.

Literature: Manthey, 1985a.

Calotes grandisquamis Guenther, 1875

HBL 145, TL 330 mm. Back uniformly green or with broad black vertical bars; an orange spot sometimes is present on each black scale; underside pale green. Six to 12 eggs are laid. Native to India (Anaimalai and Bramagherry Hills; Ponmudi, Travancore).

Literature: Smith, 1935.

Calotes jerdoni Guenther, 1870

HBL 100, TL 285 mm. Back green with yellow, orange, or brown markings; black shoulder fold present. Highlands, approximately 1800 meters, on low bushes or ferns. Mating and egg laying occur in August; up to 12 eggs are laid under moss. Assam, India (Khasi Hills); Burma (Chin

A young female *Calotes versicolor* from the Malaysian Peninsula. Photo: U. Manthey.

Hills and Maymyo); western Yunnan (China).
Literature: Smith, 1935.

Calotes liocephalus Guenther, 1872

HBL 90, TL up to 260 mm; hatchlings 26 + 58 mm (HBL + TL). No spiny scales are found on the sides of the head, the

A specimen of *Calotes versicolor*, the Brown Garden Lizard, from the Maldives. This male is about as colorful as the species gets. Photo: R. Heselhaus.

dorsal crest is low, and males have conspicuously large heads. The front of the body and the head are green or bluish green with irregular black vertical bars; the ventral side is yellow or yellowish green. Juveniles are green with dark crossbars on the olive legs and tail; the body has three whitish vertical bands. Three eggs (11 x 19 mm) are laid in August. Uplands at 400-1000 meters, on tree trunks. Sri Lanka (Peradeniya, Pandalu Oya, and Knuckles Mountains).
Literature: Erdelen, 1984.

Calotes nemoricola Jerdon, 1853

HBL male 72-145, female 64-120; TL up to 330 mm; hatchlings 25 + 51 mm (HBL + TL). Back green or brownish with indistinct dark markings. A black stripe runs from the eye to above the tympanum. The throat has black stripes, and the gular pouch in males is pink to blood red. The breeding season runs from April to September. The 8 to 16 eggs (7.5 x 12 mm) hatch after 49 to 51 days. This follower of civilization is found in gardens and trees and on the ground. The diet includes small lizards and black ants and other insects. Southern India.
Literature: Rao & Rajabai, 1972a, b.

Calotes nigrilabris Peters, 1860

HBL male 86-105, TL 270-310, female somewhat smaller; hatchlings 30 + 74 mm

Sri Lanka has many unique and sometimes colorful species of agamids, including several garden lizards. At left is *Calotes nigrilabris*, and at right is *Calotes liocephalus*. Photos: U. Manthey.

(HBL + TL). Back black in the cool of the morning, otherwise uniformly green or with white vertical bars or patches bordered with black. Sides of head of male with a broad black or brown band, in female usually with a white, black-edged stripe. Two to four eggs (11 x 17 mm) are laid in sandy soils between October and December. This species is found on the sides of roads on rocks or fence posts only in highlands at 1300-2500 meters; it requires a cloud-forest terrarium. Sri Lanka.
Literature: Annandale, 1912.

Calotes rouxi Dumeril & Bibron, 1837

HBL 77, TL 170 mm. A nape crest is present in both sexes, but the dorsal crest is only suggested in males and absent in females. There is a gular pouch only in males. Normally this lizard is brownish with dark markings and a dark shoulder fold, but during the breeding season (May to September) males become deep black with an intense red median dorsal stripe and the top of the head also is red, as are a band from the tip of the snout to the shoulder and the tip of the gular pouch.

Four to nine eggs (6 x 11 mm) are laid. Found in forests, this is an arboreal species. Southern India.
Literature: Daniel, 1983.

Ceratophora Gray, 1934

Horned Agamas: 3 species
Characteristics: The common name refers to the conspicuous rostral appendages of these fairly small arboreal agamids. They are erectile organs and contain soft, spongelike tissue surrounded by a protective covering of scales. In males the rostral horns are larger than in females. The back is covered with irregularly arranged, roof-tilelike scales of different sizes. A gular pouch and a visible tympanum are absent, as is a dorsal crest. Only a weakly developed nape crest is present.
Habits: These slow agamids are found in moist montane forests, where they live on the lower parts of tree trunks or forage for food on the ground.
Keeping: Because of destruction of habitat all species are seriously endangered. Keeping presents a few problems, such as they cannot be kept with other

Male garden lizards in breeding or territorial color may be highly iridescent. However, they also tend to attack reflections and passing shadows, thus getting bloody snouts. Photo: R. D. Bartlett.

The ultimate agamid is an adult Frilled Dragon, *Chlamydosaurus kingi*. When the frill is erected they look like nothing else in the animal kingdom. Photo: K. H. Switak.

reptiles or amphibians because they need quiet and do not tolerate stress over longer periods of time. The *Ceratophora* species feed principally on worms and smaller insects.

Range: Altitudes of 600-2100 meters, Sri Lanka.

Literature: Senanayake, 1979; Tomey, 1983a, b.

Ceratophora stoddarti Gray, 1834
Tusk-horned Agama

Description: HBL 80, TL 151 mm. *Ceratophora stoddarti* has a cylindrical, soft, smooth horn that tapers to the tip. It is located on the tip of the snout. The length of the horn is sex-dependent, being considerably smaller or absent (42 percent of the time) in females (but males without horns have been found). The small, lobelike nape crest of the male usually hangs loosely to the side, but can also be erected. Males exhibit shades of brown or green with patches of black that can form indistinct

The distinctive Scaly-horn Agama, *Ceratophora aspera*, is found only in the central highlands of Sri Lanka. Photo: Kielmann.

Few hobbyists have ever seen a living Tusk-horned Agama, *Ceratophora stoddarti*, one of the most unique Sri Lankan lizards. Photo: U. Manthey.

vertical bars on the back. In some specimens there is a bright yellow patch in the shoulder region. The horn, the throat, and the upper labials are whitish and stand out from the rest of the head coloration. Females have a brown, dark-spotted back with a lighter longitudinal dorsal band. Juveniles are brownish to light olive and have whitish V-shaped vertical bands on the head. From the occiput to the tail runs a very light, white-edged longitudinal dorsal stripe that is covered with dark spots.

Habitat and behavior: These agamids perch on tree trunks at a height of about 1 to 2 meters (40 to 80 in) in open parts of the forest. They move deliberately and hold their position at the approach of a human, since they rely on their camouflage. Juveniles are more frequently encountered on the ground. *Ceratophora stoddarti* is the only horned agama that is also found in home gardens.

In *Ceratophora tennenti* the rostral appendage is distinctly flattened and leaf-shaped. This is a male. Photo: U. Manthey.

Reproduction: Mating is "circumspect," without prior biting by the male. Usually four eggs are laid and buried in the substrate.

Notes: This lizard is a very slow eater. It needs a cloud-forest terrarium (H abt. 120, L abt. 150, D abt. 60 cm).

Range: Altitudes of 1500-2100 meters in the central highlands of Sri Lanka (cloud-forest).

Ceratophora tennenti Guenther, 1861
Leaf-horned Agama

Description: HBL 68-80, TL 135-145 mm. Both sexes have a leafshaped, laterally flattened rostral appendage that tapers to a point and is covered with many scales. When they are excited, the males erect a higher nape crest than do the females; their rostral appendage also is larger. Above the bright blue to brownish gray flanks of the male runs an olive to brownish dorsal longitudinal band. The throat varies from intense yellow to yellowish olive. The broad band that runs from the tip of the snout to the nape in some specimens, or only to the corner of the mouth in others, varies from bluish white through turquoise to brownish olive. The rostral appendage also exhibits a similar range of colors. Brownish tones predominate in females, and the lighter dorsal longitudinal band has a dark border.

Habitat and behavior: *Ceratophora tennenti* inhabits virtually the same living spaces as *Ceratophora stoddarti* and also exhibits a similarly sluggish behavior. Only when capturing prey is this agamid said to be more agile.

Notes: Cloud-forest terrarium (H abt. 120, W abt. 120, D abt. 60 cm).

Range: Altitudes of 900-1200 meters, Knuckles Mountains, Sri Lanka.

Ceratophora aspera Guenther, 1864
Scaly-horn Agama

Description: HBL male 31, female 35; TL male 44, female 45 mm; hatchlings 15 + 20 mm (HBL + TL). The horn or rostral appendage is covered with large scales and rather pine-conelike; it is larger in the male. The body is grayish brown to dark brown, the throat orange in males and orange brown in females.

Notes: It is found in pairs in montane rainforests, where it is a rather terrestrial species living on low branches or in the fallen leaves. Unlike the other species of the genus, it is extremely quick and agile when capturing prey. Two eggs are laid. Provide it with a rainforest terrarium.

Range: Central highlands of Sri Lanka.

Chelosania Gray, 1845
Chameleon Agamids: 1 species

Characteristics: *Chelosania* is characterized by a laterally flattened head and body. A gular pouch, a low nape crest, and a visible tympanum are present. The tip of the tail is blunt. Femoral and preanal pores are absent, as is the gular fold.

Habits: This agamid, which primarily lives on trees, inhabits semi-moist savannahs and gallery forests with low trees and dense shrubbery.

Keeping: A dry-forest terrarium (H abt. 100, W abt. 120, D abt. 80 cm) probably is suitable for the care of this species. A diet of insects should be offered.

Range: Northern Western Australia and Northern Territory into Queensland, Australia.

Chelosania brunnea Gray, 1845

HBL 118, TL 182 mm. Pale reddish, yellow brown, or gray, with or without dark markings. Slow movements similar to those of chameleons are typical of this species. Males intimidate and threaten other males with a raised nape crest and throat pouch. Two to nine eggs are laid from June to September; these have an incubation period of 57 to 61 days.

Chlamydosaurus Gray, 1825

Frilled Dragons: 1 species

Characteristics: The genus is easily recognized by the presence of an erectile neck frill. This collar forms a huge fold of skin underneath and on the sides of the head and is supported by a number of cartilaginous processes of the tongue bone (hyoid).

Habits: Arboreal. Fleeing Frilled Dragons display an unusual form of locomotion on the ground: They run on only their hind legs. *Chlamydosaurus* inhabits dry forests and wooded steppes. Its natural diet consists of insects, smaller lizards, and ants.

Keeping: Unplanted dry-forest terrarium (H abt. 140, W abt. 200, D abt. 70 cm) with upright branches.

Range: Northern and northeastern Australia and southern New Guinea.

Chlamydosaurus kingi Gray, 1825

HBL male 220-260, TL 440-550 mm; female somewhat smaller; hatchlings 135-160 mm TL. A small nape crest of slightly enlarged scales is present. There are 6 to 20 preanal and femoral pores. The back is gray, brown, orange brown, or almost black, usually with a dark reticulation that can form irregular vertical bars. The neck frill is yellow to black, often with bright orange and red tones. After a month of mild hibernation (20°C [68°F], 17°C [63°F] at night), three clutches of 8 to 14 eggs are laid at monthly intervals. At 28.5°C (83°F) hatching occurs after 85 to 90 days. The young can be reared together in a large terrarium at first, but they must be separated after about four months.

Literature: Reisinger, 1992.

Seldom seen outside its native Australia, *Chelosania brunnea* is known as the Chameleon Agamid or Chameleon Dragon. Photo: K. H. Switak.

Frilled Dragons, *Chlamydosaurus kingi*, once were a rarity in the terrarium hobby, but today they have become relatively common and affordable. Young specimens (above) have smaller crests and frills than adults (below). Photos: R. D. Bartlett.

An adult Chameleon Dragon, *Chelosania brunnea*, from Kakadu National Park, Australia. Photo: K. H. Switak.

Cophotis Peters, 1861

Earless Agamas: 1 species

Characteristics: The back of the laterally flattened body is covered with irregularly arranged, shinglelike scales of variable size. The tympanum is not visible. The Earless Agama has nape and dorsal crests as well as a small gular pouch. The tail is prehensile.

Habits: These arboreal agamids inhabit moist montane forests. They prefer the lower regions of the trees, but also can be found in bushes and hedges within villages.

Keeping: Give these agamas a heavily planted cloud-forest or rainforest terrarium (H abt. 100, L abt. 140, D abt. 50 cm) with thin branches. They feed on insects.

Range: Altitudes of 600-2100 meters in the central highlands of Sri Lanka.

Cophotis ceylanica Peters, 1861

Sri Lankan Earless Agama

Description: HBL male 60-66, female 67; TL male 80-85, female 67 mm; hatchlings 20 + 24 mm (HBL + TL). The nape crest, which is not constantly raised, consists of three or four serrate scales and usually is separated from the similar dorsal crest. Depending on the level of excitement, males can change their coloration, various shades of brown and green predominating, often forming irregular vertical bands. Juveniles and females appear light gray with brown banding.

Habitat and behavior: These slow agamids exhibit a pronounced threat and submissive behavior.

Reproduction: *Cophotis ceylanica* is the only livebearing (ovoviviparous) arboreal agamid. The number of young varies between two and eight.

Notes: According to Kaestle, several males can be kept together, but this is not generally recommended. When two males and one female have been kept together, wounds from bites have resulted. Besides other insects, they are especially fond of bees and wasps, which are always seized by the front (stingless) end. Pregnant females and juveniles, in particular, must be given abundant doses of calcium.

Literature: Kaestle, 1966; Tomey, 1982.

"Cophotis" [Undescribed genus, Moody, 1980]: 1 species

Characteristics: Broad, roof-tilelike scales arranged in irregular vertical rows cover the back of the laterally strongly flat-

The Frilled Dragon, *Chlamydosaurus kingi*, is famous for spreading its broad frill and running away on its hind legs when frightened. Photo: R. D. Bartlett.

The large scales that look like pinecone scales in combination with the broad white lip and shoulder stripe are good identification characters for the Sri Lankan Earless Agama, *Cophotis ceylanica*. The absence of a tympanum is not always obvious. Photo: U. Manthey.

tened body. On the tip of the snout is a hornlike appendage. A large scale marks the position of the tympanum. A gular pouch is present. Elongated, pointed scales form a crest above the eye. The dorsal crest, which is separated from the nape crest, ends on the tail.

Habits: No information is available on living specimens of these dragons in miniature.

Reproduction: Egg-layers.

Keeping: Judging by the localities in which they have been found, heavily planted cloud-forest terraria would be suitable for keeping them. They probably are arboreal insectivores.

Range: Sumatra and Java.

"Cophotis" sumatrana (Hubrecht, 1879)
Indonesian Earless Agama

Description: HBL male 75, female 77-81; TL male 115, female 103-119 mm. The thin, soft rostral horn of the male is about 5 mm high; the horn of the female is lower. The eye crest consists of six or seven elongated scales. A group of nine spines over 4 mm long forms a nape crest that is clearly separated from the dorsal crest. The latter is low in males or only suggested in females, but crest scales

are absent only on the tip of the tail. The back and tail exhibit broad, dark vertical bars. The entire dorsal side probably is colored green in life.

Range: Padang?, western Sumatra; Bogor and Pengalengan, western Java.

Coryphophylax Fitzinger, 1843
Nicobar Forest Dragons: 1 species

Characteristics: In contrast to the similar species of the genus *Gonocephalus*, the tail breaks off easily and regenerates. The two genera are not easy to tell apart by external characters.

Habits: These agamids are closely tied to forests. They are extremely fast, climb skillfully up tree trunks, and when fleeing jump from tree to tree.

Keeping: A rainforest terrarium (H abt. 150, L abt. 150, D abt. 70 cm) with vertical climbing branches should suffice.

Range: Nicobar and Andaman Islands.

Coryphophylax subcristatus (Blyth, 1860)

Description: HBL male 100, TL 270 mm, female smaller. The occiput has enlarged conical scales, and the dorsal scales are very small, keeled, mixed with larger ones. For-

The rarely seen *Coryphophylax subcristatus*. Photo: Grossmann.

mation of the dorsal crest is dependent on age and population. The nape crest of adult males consists of triangular scales on curved folds of skin. The dorsal crest consists of identical scales that are somewhat separated from the nape crest and continue onto the tail. Juveniles and females are uniformly greenish or have black markings; males have variable reticulate markings or dark brown vertical stripes on the flanks, the spaces between them yellow or red. The gular pouch has a yellow/red/black pattern.

Cryptagama Witten, 1984

Fringe-lip Agamas: 1 species

Characteristics: *Cryptagama* differs from most other agamas in its dorsoventrally compressed, extremely flattened body and head. The limbs are short, and the tail, which is blunt at the tip, is shorter than the head-body length. Over the entire dorsal side, larger tubercular scales mix with smaller scales. The upper labial scales form a scalloped border. The tympanum is visible. Males are distin-

guished from females by the conspicuous hemipenis pouches.

Habits: These small terrestrial agamas live on sandy loam and laterite soils covered with thick shrubbery and boulders. They lie in ambush for small insects, especially ants. When danger threatens the lizards often rely on their mimetic abilities or disappear into cracks in the ground or under large rocks, where they also stay in the hottest and driest times.

Keeping: For a pair, an arid terrarium with the dimensions H abt. 60, W abt. 80, D abt. 50 cm is sufficient. It is furnished with marly sand and fairly large rocks, as well as a gnarled branch and a drinking bowl. Small insects and ants make up the main part of the diet. The lizards should occasionally be offered vegetable foods.

Range: Western Australia and the Northern Territory in the vicinity of Hals Creek as well as Wolf Creek Crater to Wave Hill.

Cryptagama aurita (Storr, 1981)

Description: HBL 45, TL 40 mm. The lizards are mostly pale brown to brick red and are covered with small brown specks on the head and back; the belly is whitish. The tail has several irregular dark brown to brownish gray bands. They are egg-layers.

Ctenophorus Fitzinger, 1843

Australian Dragons: 22 species and 12 subspecies

As a function of their different habits, this endemic Australian genus has been divided into 4 groups (Ehmann, 1992).

Ctenophrus decresi group, Crevice Dragons. Six species: *Ctenophorus decresi*, *Ctenophorus fionni*, *Ctenophorus ornatus*, *Ctenophorus rufescens*, *Ctenophorus vadnappa*, *Ctenophorus yinnietharra*.

Characteristics: These dragons reach a HBL of 80-96 mm. Their body is clearly flattened dorsoventrally. The tympanum is surrounded by spiny scales. The lively coloration of the males makes it possible to distinguish easily the species and sexes. Because of a plain brownish to brownish gray color with weak dark specks and markings, the females of the various species look very similar.

Almost never available because they are protected in their native Australia, *Ctenophorus decresi* is an attractive but very aggressive lizard. Photo: U. Manthey.

Habits: Crevice dragons are terrestrial agamids that inhabit rugged rocky landscapes, in the cracks of which they find refuge. They feed on insects.

Keeping: An arid terrarium (H abt. 130, L abt. 130, D abt. 70 cm) with a rocky rear wall is suitable.

Ctenophorus decresi Dumeril & Bibron, 1837

Description: HBL male 80, TL 168 mm. The small dorsal scales are usually interspersed with a few somewhat larger tubercular scales on the flanks. Females and juveniles exhibit a brownish or gray, dark-speckled back, and dark, wavy stripes can be present on the flanks. The chin and neck have dark speckling, and the belly is pale. The back of males is brownish or blue-gray. The dark head and flanks of the front part of the body exhibit white, yellow, or orange stripes up to the tympanum. The throat and the breast are bright orange in northern populations, bluish in southern ones.

Habitat and behavior: *Ctenophorus decresi* lives in moist to arid regions on insular mountains and in valleys where ponds or small streams are often present. Juveniles inhabit sandy areas between talus, away from the locales of the adults. Populations of the southernmost part of the range (Cape Jervis and Kangaroo Island) overwinter for a month in crevices.

Reproduction: The breeding season begins in the Australian spring. In early summer the females lay three to eight eggs that need 53 to 79 days to develop.

Notes: A terrarium can only house a single male because of aggressive interactions.

Range: Eastern South Australia, Kangaroo Island, Mount Lofty, Flinders Range, as well as Olary Spur to Nonntharangee Range in northern New South Wales.

Literature: Houston, 1974.

Ctenophorus maculatus group, Sand Dragons.

5 species, 12 subspecies: *Ctenophorus femoralis, Ctenophorus fordi, Ctenophorus isolepis, Ctenophorus maculatus, Ctenophorus rubens.*

Characteristics: Slender bodies (HBL 55-85 mm) with long tails characterize the small sand dragons. Males are identified by their dark ventral markings, which extend onto the flanks in several species.

Habits: Purely terrestrial agamids, these lizards prefer sandy habitats with dense plant growth that offers them protection from the hot midday sun and cover at night. They feed on ants and seldom live longer than a year in the wild.

Keeping: The first attempts should be made in an arid terrarium (H abt. 80, L abt. 120, D abt. 60 cm) with a deep layer of sand (about 20 to 30 cm, 8 to 12 in) and a few clumps of dry grass. It is not known if these ant specialists also eat other insects.

Ctenophorus femoralis (Storr, 1965)

Notes: HBL 55, TL 65 mm. These small lizards are an inconspicuous reddish above with small dark or light specks or dots. They live on red sandy soils, closely tied to *Triodia* grasses. In addition to ants they also eat other small insects. The species is found only in the vicinity of Exmouth Gulf, Western Australia.

Ctenophorus reticulatus group, Netted Dragons. 7 species: *Ctenophorus clayi, Ctenophorus gibba, Ctenophorus maculosus, Ctenophorus nuchalis, Ctenophorus pictus, Ctenophorus reticulatus, Ctenophorus salinarum.*

Characteristics: Relatively short legs and tails, broad heads, and a visibly dorsoventrally flattened body characterize the group. The tympanum is small or is hidden under scales. The HBL is 60-115 mm.

Habits: These agamids of the lowlands retreat into burrows in sandy soils that several of the species seal to gain protection from heat, rain, and predators. Though *Ctenophorus maculosus* feeds only on ants and other insects, the other species also eat flowers, leaves, and fruits.

Keeping: The lively netted dragons are quite trusting in arid terraria (H abt. 100, L abt. 120, D abt. 80 cm). Overfeeding must be avoided. Imitation termite nests, dead branches, a few rocks, and dried grasses are suitable as decorations.

Ctenophorus nuchalis **(de Vis, 1888)**
Central Netted Dragon
Description: HBL male 115, TL 170 mm, female clearly smaller; hatchlings 50-65 mm TL. A small crest of scales is present on the nape. Fairly large scales, in part arranged into vertical rows, mix with small smooth or weakly keeled dorsal scales. Independent of age, both sexes exhibit the same coloration: a reddish to blackish brown reticulate pattern covers the head and body, and a light dorsal median line extends between large specks with light borders and is surrounded by dark spots on both sides.

Habitat and behavior: *Ctenophorus nuchalis* lives in grassy or open shrubby steppes on sandy soils. In certain regions each termite mound is occupied by a dragon. When danger threatens they disappear like a flash into their holes in the ground or under bushes or grasses.

Reproduction: During the breeding season from October to December, pairs often lie close together. Females take an active role in courtship. Four to six weeks after copulation they lay two to six eggs that, depending on temperature, require an incubation period of 55 to 79 days. About half of the youngsters die in the first few

The Central Netted Dragon, *Ctenophorus nuchalis*, is an attractive Australian agamid. Like the other species of the genus, they can be very aggressive. Photo: Eidenmueller.

weeks, but the others usually develop without problems. After about four weeks they establish hierarchies and the males must be separated.

Notes: The breeding group should never include more than one pair, because even cies exhibit a small dorsal crest. Their coloration is less adapted to the environment than that of the other groups.

Habits: These agamids inhabit loamy soils with gravel and larger rocks in arid to semi-arid regions of the plains and uplands.

A male *Ctenophorus pictus*, one of the very colorful species of a genus that is virtually unknown outside of Australia. Photo: K. H. Switak.

females establish a hierarchy. In the natural biotope only about 2 percent of the young survive the first year of life.

Range: Western and central Australia, from the coast to western Queensland and western New South Wales.

Literature: Klages, 1982.

***Ctenophorus scutulatus* group**, Dashing Dragons. 4 species: *Ctenophorus caudicinctus, Ctenophorus cristatus, Ctenophorus mckenziei, Ctenophorus scutulatus.*

Characteristics: These agile ground-dwellers have a rounded body with long tails compared to the other groups. Several spe-

The vegetation varies from open forest to low shrubby landscapes. Southern species undergo a period of reduced activity in the Australian fall and winter. When danger threatens they flee like a flash over long stretches, sometimes only on the hind legs, until the enemy is out of sight. Their diet consists of flying insects, which they catch on the run and by jumping. Some species live only two years.

Keeping: A large arid terrarium (H abt. 100, L abt. 150, D abt. 80 cm) is necessary for the care of these agamids. The substrate should consist of a mixture of loam, sand, and gravel with a few larger rocks.

The Central Netted Dragon, *Ctenophorus nuchalis*. Photo: Z. Takacs.

A long cork tube can serve as a climbing branch and hiding place. In the acclimation phase the terrarium glass must be treated so that it is opaque, so that the agamids do not run into it.

Ctenophorus cristatus (Gray, 1841)
Crested Dragon
Description: HBL male 110, female 67; TL male 260, female 125 mm. Across the nape, back, and a part of the tail runs a low spiny crest. Parallel to it are two folds of skin with enlarged scales, the folds ending in the middle of the body. Males exhibit cream or red-orange colors on the head, front legs, and body along with black markings. The remaining gray to gray-brown parts of the body are covered with inconspicuous dark or light specks. The posterior three-quarters of the tail is banded with alternating black, brown, and creamy orange. Interrupted black dorsolateral stripes extend back from the eye over the front half of the body. Black markings stand out on the light belly. Females have a gray coloration that appears darker on the back and contains faint markings. Juveniles resemble females but have a paler belly.

Habitat and behavior: *Ctenophorus cristatus* inhabits both arid and semi-arid regions with loamy soils and forested and shrubby landscapes that often are strewn with large rocks. They hibernate in the Australian fall and winter. During the rest of the year males, in particular, perch in exposed places where they can get a good view of their surroundings. When danger threatens they take refuge in hollow trees or in deep (40 to 100 cm, 16 to 40 in), steep burrows in the soil. Males intimidate other males with their bright breeding coloration and distended gular pouches and also whip their tail. Their principal foods are small insects and skinks.

Reproduction: From October to January, two to five eggs are laid. The incubation period is 53 to 75 days.

Range: Southern Western and South Australia.

Literature: Pianka, 1971.

Dendragama Doria, 1888
Sumatran Tree Dragons: 1 species
Characteristics: The body is laterally flattened. Both sexes have a gular pouch, a visible tympanum, and a nape crest that is separated from the dorsal crest. The crest scales are not close together; there is a clear separation between them. These characters and the form and size of the distinct dorsal scales clearly distinguish *Dendragama* from the similar genera *Calotes, Pseudocalotes,* and *Bronchocela.*

Habits: Based on our own observations, this highland agamid prefers semi-shaded bushes near streams, outside of forests, but it does not avoid human habitation either. During the dry season considerably more males than females are seen.

Keeping: A heavily planted cloud-forest terrarium (H abt. 100, W abt. 200, D abt. 60 cm) with thin branches will do. Dry and rainy seasons must be simulated. These agamids are insectivores.

Range: Northern and western Sumatra.

Dendragama boulengeri Doria, 1888
Description: HBL male 65-72, female 70; TL male 144-158, female 146-149 mm. Four to seven spiny scales form the nape crest on a ridge of skin. The triangular dorsal crest scales extend to the base of the tail. The back of the male usually is bright green, the sides showing dark netting. Short, in part indistinct, dark vertical bands adorn the back. In the shoulder region, on both sides of the body, is a black, elongated, yellow-bordered patch. The green back can take on a brown hue quite rapidly, and then the formerly black shoulder patch stands out conspicuously lighter. This pronounced change in color has yet be observed in females. Otherwise the sexes exhibit similar coloration and markings, only the green of the back is less bright and contains more shades of brown in the female. Both sexes may have a light or dark ventral side. The iris is a gleaming greenish blue (males) or brown (females).

Reproduction: A female from the Karo Mountains laid four eggs (8 x 14 mm) during the dry season in March.

Range: Mount Singalang, 2800 meters, western Sumatra; Vulkan Sinabung, Brastagi, Karo Mountains, 1400 meters; near Lake Toba, 1200 meters, Mount Simbolon, all in northern Sumatra.

Diporiphora Gray, 1842

Two-lined Dragons: 16 species

Characteristics: These small to medium-sized terrestrial agamids are small-headed and slender with long legs and a long tail. They have a visible tympanum, preanal pores, and rarely two femoral pores. Usually, however, nape and dorsal crests are absent. The homogeneous dorsal scales usually are keeled. Because *Diporiphora* species vary little in markings, size, form, and scale arrangement, it is difficult to distinguish the individual species. The bright vertical banding of younger animals is lost with age.

Habits: The genus *Diporiphora* is widely distributed in Australia and is not confined to a particular biotope. Some species hide during the hottest time of day, others are active at night on warm roads. They feed primarily on insects.

Keeping: Because the individual species inhabit different biotopes, uniform keeping conditions are not possible. The species *Diporiphora albilabris, Diporiphora bennetti,* and *Diporiphora magna,* for example, prefer regions with water courses, whereas other species are more adapted to arid habitats.

Range: Australia and southern New Guinea.

A male Sumatran Tree Dragon, *Dendragama boulengeri*. Photo: U. Manthey.

Diporiphora bennetti (Gray, 1845)

Description: HBL 65-80, TL up to 180 mm. A small nape crest and a weakly developed gular fold as well as two to six preanal pores are present. The coloration of the back varies through different shades of brown. Younger specimens exhibit dark vertical bars on a usually gray vertebral stripe between light dorsolateral stripes. The dark brown flanks are speckled with gray, white, or yellow. On the shoulder is a dark patch that generally continues to be present in older specimens, whereas the remaining markings become indistinct or disappear entirely. In the mating season the head, breast, hips, hindlegs, and base of the tail turn orange in males.

Habitat and behavior: These agamids often live near water courses on sandy soils with rubble and sandstone on which spiny grasses and clumps of other grasses as well as trees grow. The climate is hot and moderately humid.

Reproduction: The female lays four or five eggs in January.

Notes: A dry-forest terrarium (H abt. 100, L abt. 120, D abt. 80 cm) furnished with a few rocks and diagonal climbing branches, as well as a small water course, should be suitable for keeping this species, but there are few published experiences.

Range: Kimberley region of Western Australia and the Northern Territory, Australia.

Draco Linnaeus, 1758

Flying Dragons: 20 species and 19 subspecies

Characteristics: Distinctive for the lively *Draco* species are two large, often colorful folds of skin on the flanks that are supported by elongated movable ribs.

Diporiphora australis, a two-lined dragon from Queensland, Australia. Photo: R. W. Van Devender.

Other dermal sails (skin projections) are located on the sides of the neck. The gular pouch often is long and narrow, sometimes crescent-shaped.

Habits: The dermal sails usually are folded along the body. Only when a flying dragon jumps from a tree do the lobes of skin spread and enable the dragon to make steered gliding flights. Distances of about 50 meters (160 ft) can be covered. They always sail to another tree and land with the head up. Not infrequently this tree is already occupied by another male, which immediately defends his territory.

found in open forests as well as dense rainforests of the lowlands and highlands. They feed almost exclusively on ants and termites, which they consume in large numbers. The coloration of the "wings" is variable and often differs in males and females. The available descriptions of the coloration sometime contain contradictory claims. Therefore, the identification of some *Draco* is extraordinarily difficult.

Keeping: Depending on provenance, dry-forest or rainforest terraria (H abt. 200, L abt. 400, D abt. 70 cm) with a number of thick, vertical branches are

The gliding ribs are easily seen in this specimen of the flying dragon *Draco blanfordi*. Note also the many conical scales at the back of the head that are important in identification. Photo: K. T. Nemuras.

The body is positioned at right angles, and through head nodding as well as the rapid, abrupt expansion of the colorful gular pouch he tries to intimidate the intruder, which subsequently reacts in the same fashion. After some time one of the two flees on a spiral path up the tree and is followed immediately by the other until it is again stopped by threat displays. The chase lasts until one of the rivals leaves the tree. Flying dragons are

suitable. Although smaller to medium-sized specimens often are seen, we must advise against keeping them. In addition to the large space requirements, the diet presents additional problems.

Reproduction: Almost all species lay one to four (rarely six) eggs. As far as is known, the incubation period is only 30 to about 70 days.

Literature: Inger, 1983; Lazell, 1992; Musters, 1983.

***Draco blanfordi blanfordi* Boulenger, 1885**

Notes: HBL male 120-134, female up to 113 mm. Flight membrane brownish above with fine light longitudinal stripes, yellow below. Thai/Malaysian Peninsula and somewhat to the north. *Draco blanfordi indochinensis*—Cambodia, Vietnam; *Draco blanfordi norvilli*—Assam, northern India, and northern Burma.

with dark spots, the female orange with yellow spots. Thai/Malaysian Peninsula, Borneo, Sumatra. *Draco fimbriatus hennigi*—Java.

***Draco maculatus maculatus* (Gray, 1845)**

Notes: HBL male up to 87, female up to 80 mm. Body gray to brown. Flight membrane red above, yellowish toward body,

The patagium or flight membrane of most species of flying dragon shows distinctive color patterns, but often the pattern varies geographically and with age and sex. This is a species thought to be related to *Draco maculatus*. Photo: R. D. Bartlett.

***Draco dussumieri* Dumeril & Bibron, 1837**

Notes: HBL male 78-86, female 86-97 mm. Skin between the ribs reddish black with yellow spots, gular pouch yellow. Reproduces during the monsoon rains. Southern India.

***Draco fimbriatus fimbriatus* Kuhl, 1820**

Notes: HBL male 90-112, female 102-117 mm. Body brown to gray with dark markings. Flight membrane colored like the body above, the male light gray below

with black spots arranged in longitudinal lines; the coloration of the dorsal side shines through below. Burma, western Thailand, Thai/Malaysian Peninsula. *Draco maculatus haasei*—eastern Thailand, Cambodia, southern Vietnam; *Draco maculatus whiteheadi*—northern Vietnam, Hainan.

***Draco melanopogon* Boulenger, 1887**

Notes: HBL male up to 85, female up to 93 mm. Body greenish with dark markings. Flight membrane black above with numerous yellow spots; gular pouch black. Usually two eggs are laid. Thai/Malay-

Compare the color pattern on the flight membranes of this *Draco lineatus* with that of the species on the facing page. Unfortunately, the life colors of most *Draco* are poorly known. Photo: S. Minton.

Draco volans is one of the most familiar names applied to a flying dragon, but it probably represents a group of many species. Notice the long orange central gular pouch typical of many flying dragons. Photo: R. G. Sprackland.

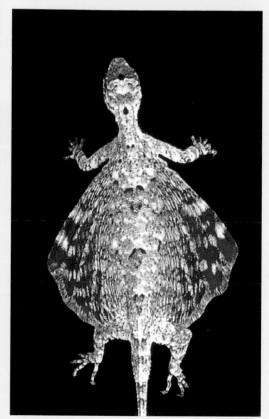

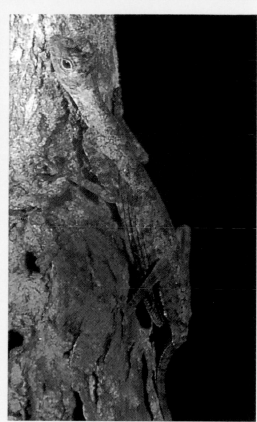

Top Left: *Draco volans sumatranus* displaying the flight membrane. Top Right: *Draco melanopogon*. Photos: U. Manthey.

Below: A male *Draco maculatus*. Photo: R. D. Bartlett.

sian Peninsula, Sumatra, Borneo, and numerous surrounding islands.

Draco quinquefasciatus Hardwicke & Gray, 1827

Notes: HBL male up to 105, female 106 mm. Body variable, brownish, yellowish green, or gray, sometimes with bluish specks. Flight membrane yellow, orange, or reddish above with five black cross-bands; in the middle is a transverse row of light spots. Thai/Malaysian Peninsula, Sumatra, Borneo.

Draco volans volans Linnaeus, 1758

Notes: HBL male up to 82, female up to 96 mm. Body gray with dark pattern. Flight membrane gray, covered with black and light specks. Java and Bali. *Draco volans boschmai*—Indonesian islands of Lombok, Sumbawa, Komodo, Rintja, Sumba, Adunara, Flores, Sulawesi; *Draco volans reticulatus*—Philippines; *Draco volans sumatranus*—Thai/Malaysian Peninsula, Sumatra, Borneo, Palawan, as well as numerous surrounding islands; *Draco volans timoriensis*—Indonesian islands of Timor, Roti, Alos, Semur, Wetar.

Gonocephalus Kaup, 1825

Angleheads: 17 species and 2 subspecies

Characteristics: The name *Gonocephalus* literally means angular or square head. It refers both to the curve of the eyebrow and the bony ridge between the eye and nostril (canthus rostralis) that give the head a solid, boxy appearance. The body is laterally flattened. These agamids, depending on the species, reach a HBL of 90-170 mm and a maximum total length of 430 mm. A throat and shoulder fold, gular pouch, nape crest, and visible tympanum are always present in both sexes. The dorsal scales are small and homogeneous or mixed with larger ones.

Habits: In rainforests of the lowlands and uplands, angleheads often inhabit the uppermost region of the rainforest giants, so they are hard to collect. They like to roost on the tips of thin branches. Based on field observations, they do not travel too far from flowing water and also defecate there.

Keeping: In a rainforest terrarium (H abt. 150, L abt. 150, D abt. 70 cm) with

Flying dragons have many areas of specialized scales on the body. Notice in this specimen of *Draco* the spiny scales on the legs and at the edges of the tail, as well as the very large scales on the folded gular pouch and in front of the eye. Photo: W. Wuster.

Few lizards can match a male *Gonocephalus chamaeleontinus* for the unusual appearance of the spiny crests. Notice the pointed "eyebrows" typical of this group and source of the name "anglehead." Photo: U. Manthey.

robust plants as well as vertical thick and thin branches, angleheads can be kept for many years and also are relatively easy to breed. They eat larger insects, occasionally nestling mice, and some of them also take earthworms. The peacefulness of these agamids (with the exception of *Gonocephalus grandis*) makes it possible to keep two or three species in a large terrarium without negatively influencing breeding success. Wild-caught specimens often need a rather long acclimation period during which they occasionally react with panic to hasty movements by the keeper.

Range: Altitudes of 0-1600 meters, Thai/Malaysian Peninsula (south of the Isthmus of Kra), Sumatra, Java, Borneo, and the Philippines, as well as a number of small islands in the Sunda Archipelago.

Literature: Manthey & Denzer, 1991b.

Gonocephalus belli (Dumeril & Bibron, 1837)

Description: HBL male 125-150, female

The juvenile *Gonocephalus chamaeleontinus* lacks the distinctive nape crest of the adult male. Photo: U. Manthey.

A female *Gonocephalus belli*. Photo: U. Manthey.

105-120; TL male 260-340, female 225-250 mm; hatchlings 25-32 + 50-52 mm (HBL + TL). The continuous dorsal crest is formed of tall lanceolate scales that regularly decrease in height toward the tail. The coloration of adult males varies depending on the population and degree of excitement, and they may be blackish, dirty yellowish, umber-colored, or greenish with dark reticulate markings. On the gular pouch either dark blue to lilac dominates or, just as in females, dark blue with pink specks. The back of the female is overlain with brownish or reddish tones that can contain yellow spots or short yellow bars. Juveniles, depending on the population, exhibit inconspicuous brownish gray or intense reddish tones with yellow spots. The eyes are blue (adult males) or brown (juveniles and females).

Habitat and behavior: *Gonocephalus belli* lives on thick tree trunks near flowing water. When disturbed they run up the trunk, where they are almost impossible to observe.

Reproduction: These angleheads reach sexual maturity at a head-body length of about 90-100 mm. The iris of the male then turns from brown through gray blue to a bright blue color. The male courts the female by displaying a dark blue, inflated gular pouch along with the usual nodding of the head and a peculiar sideways turning of the head. In so doing the head is turned to the

Identification of angleheads may be very difficult because few specimens are imported and there are few reliable discussions of the genus in life. Also, males and females often differ greatly in cresting and coloration. These specimens are identified as *Gonocephalus doriae abbotti*. A male is shown above (photo by R. D. Bartlett), a female below (photo by P. Freed).

side jerkily with two or three pauses, which gives the impression that in the intermediate positions the head "snaps into position." At intervals of two to three months, the female lays and then buries three to five eggs (11-11.5 x 18-20.5 mm). At an average temperature of 20.5°C (69°F), the incubation period is seven months; at an average of 23 to 25°C (83 to 77°F) it is only 136 days. Just before hatching the eggs reach a size of 17-17.8 x 28.9-29.5 mm.

Notes: Wild-caught specimens usually need only a short acclimation period, during which they are reclusive and sometimes eat poorly. Animals that have been kept in the terrarium for a longer time exhibit no shyness and often are the first at the food. Communal keeping with other angleheads of the same size (except for *Gonocephalus grandis*) or prickle-napes presents no problems.

Range: Altitudes of 0-1000 meters, Thai/Malaysian Peninsula and Pinang Island.
Literature: Manthey & Denzer, 1992b.

Gonocephalus chamaeleontinus (Laurenti, 1768)

Description: HBL male 115-170, female 115-150; TL male 190-280, female 170-240 mm; the Java population is smaller. Hatchlings 30-34 + 36-46 mm (HBL + TL). Characteristic of this species is the short, massive head with high, angled curve of the eyebrow, which ends in an acute angle (for which the genus was named). The triangular to lanceolate dorsal crest scales are positioned on a curved fold of skin in the nape region. On the flanks, larger tubercular scales often are mixed with smaller granulated ones. The ventral scales are absolutely smooth. Green in various nuances usually dominates on the back; it can be broken up by yellow spots, lines, and short cross-bars as well as a dark netting. Blue stripes decorate the large gular pouch. Despite the strongly thickened base of the tail of males, sex determination is not easy. Brown specimens without any shades of green also have been described from Sumatra. Older females from this island are characterized by very high nape crest scales.

Habitat and behavior: Based on observations on Sumatra and Tioman, these agamids perch both on vertical tree trunks

of medium circumference and on diagonal branches or lianas. A stream was never more than 100 meters (330 ft) away. The active period is limited primarily to the early morning and late evening hours.

Reproduction: Sexual maturity is reached after about three years. In the course of a year four clutches are laid at intervals of two to four and a half months. The clutch size is three to five eggs (12-13 x 21-24 mm) and the incubation period is 81 to 97 days at 23 to 25°C (73 to 77°F) and 134 days at 19 to 25°C (66 to 77°F). Shortly before hatching the eggs reach a size of 18-19 x 28-33 mm.

Notes: Adult *Gonocephalus chamaeleontinus* are very quiet and peaceful angleheads. This is also true of juveniles and subadults outside of feeding times. Besides insects, they also accept earthworms and pinkie mice. When the animals are placed together in a terrarium, two males can be kept together with two females. In the rearing of the youngsters it should be kept in mind that they should not be fed with wax worms or they will not accept any other foods with the exception of winged ants. It is better first to acclimate them to crickets and earthworms, even though as a result it will occasionally take somewhat longer for them to feed independently.

Range: Palau Tioman, western Malaysia; Sumatra and a few nearby islands; Natuna Islands; Java to an altitude of about 500 meters.
Literature: Manthey & Denzer, 1992c.

Gonocephalus borneensis (Schlegel, 1848)

Notes: HBL male 118-136, female 90-130; TL male 261-310, female 215-275 mm. The crest of males is made up of high, closely spaced, lanceolate scales and runs without interruption to the base of the tail. Females have a clearly higher nape crest than dorsal crest, the crest height decreasing sharply in the front half of the body so that in the rear half only low triangular scales remain. Subadult males have a brown or green coloration and dark reticulate markings. The gular pouches of both sexes are pale, with dark, broken stripes. Females are similar in coloration to female

Various angleheads, genus *Gonocephalus*. Top left: A female *G. grandis*. Top right: A female *G. borneensis*. Bottom: A male *G. grandis* showing the pendant gular pouch and the blue and yellow spotted pattern on the lower side. Photos: U. Manthey.

An adult *Gonocephalus* species. Often incorrectly called *G. grandis*, this species lacks the broad angled bars across the back in females and the blue and yellow pattern on the side of males, both features that occur in the real *G. grandis*. Photo: P. Freed.

Gonocephalus belli or green with dark netting. Found in the vicinity of flowing water on thick tree trunks or lianas, they often flee to hiding places on the ground and are not sedentary. Four eggs, 22 mm long, are laid every three months. Borneo. **Literature:** Manthey & Denzer, 1982, 1992a.

Gonocephalus doriae doriae Peters, 1871

Notes: HBL male 115-132, female 100-125; TL male 177-189, female 134-178 mm. Its overall appearance resembles *Gonocephalus chamaeleontinus*, but the scales of the nape crest are not single, high, and lanceolate, but rather overlapping, low, and slightly crescent-shaped. The dorsal scalation may be with or without scattered larger scales. The hemipenis pouches are weakly developed. Males are red with dark and light specks or greenish to olive. Juveniles and females often are almost uniformly green. This species is very peaceful in the terrarium, which should be modeled after a lowland rainforest. *Gonocephalus doriae abbotti*—Thai/Malaysian Peninsula (HBL male 130-160, female 130-140; TL male up to 220, female up to 205 mm); *Gonocephalus doriae doriae*—Borneo.
Literature: Manthey & Denzer, 1992c.

Gonocephalus grandis (Gray, 1845)

Notes: HBL male 134-160, female 115-137; TL male 345-427, female 305-365 mm; hatchlings 32-35 + 48-65 mm (HBL + TL). Males have high, lanceolate scales on a curved nape crest and a separate dorsal crest of scales of the same kind; females have only a fold of skin forming the nape crest. The male's back is various shades of green to almost black, the flanks blue with yellow spots, and the gular pouch yellow to red with blue stripes. The female is brownish, greenish, anthracite, or almost black above with light, V-shaped vertical bands; flank coloration is similar to that of males. Juveniles are colored like females but have pale flanks with dark netting. These angleheads are found on trees and bushes directly along flowing water, and juveniles and females often are found by and in water. Sexual maturity is reached after about 20 months. One to six eggs (10-11 x 21-26 mm) are laid at intervals of one to three months

and hatch after a period of 75 to 90 days. They cannot be kept with other lizards because they are very aggressive and prone to bite. The species is found on the Thai/Malaysian Peninsula and the islands of Pinang and Tioman, plus Borneo and Sumatra and surrounding islands.
Literature: Manthey & Denzer, 1991c.

Gonocephalus kuhli (Schlegel, 1848)

Notes: HBL 70-100, TL 155-185 mm; hatchlings 30 + 46 mm (HBL + TL). It is similar to *Gonocephalus chamaeleontinus*, but the nape crest is lower, smaller dorsal scales are always mixed with numerous larger tubercular scales, the ventral scales are convex, and males have very pronounced hemipenis pouches. Coloration is variable, principally green, often with whitish specks on the head and a band of the same color on the shoulder that varies in form and size. In some cases there are yellow or red vertical bands on the back. Four eggs (12-14 x 21-22 mm) are laid in January. It is more common at higher altitudes up to about 1600 meters than in lowlands. A native of Sumatra and Java. **Literature:** Manthey & Denzer, 1992c.

Gonocephalus lacunosus Manthey & Denzer, 1991

Notes: HBL male 125-145, female 125-138; TL male 220-270, female 200-210 mm. Males have a dorsal crest of lanceolate scales pointing slightly to the rear, not touching at the base, and separated from the nape crest. Females have a nape crest similar to that of the male and a dorsal crest of low triangular scales clearly separated from one another. This species has a robust appearance and the tail is extremely flattened laterally. Males are dirty green to dark gray, with enlarged scales on the flanks greenish or yellowish; the head and gular pouch may have turquoise markings. Females are dark green or dark gray, sometimes with brownish red vertical bars, the gular pouch and head often with turquoise markings. It is found in montane forests above 1000 meters, usually near streams on thin trees or on the ground; it hides in holes. In the cloud-forest terrarium it is very quiet, shy, and withdrawn. Seven or eight eggs are laid. Northern Sumatra.

A trio of male *Gonocephalus* species. Top left: *G. doriae*. Top right: *G. robinsoni*. Bottom: *G. liogaster*. Notice the brilliant blue eye found in many species of this genus and *Hypsilurus*. Photos: U. Manthey.

Gonocephalus liogaster (Guenther, 1872)

Notes: HBL male 120-140, female 95-120; TL male 290-320, female 220-260 mm; hatchlings 32-53 mm. Males have a continuous nape and dorsal crest of tall, lanceolate scales; the crest continuously loses height toward the tail and ends at the base of the tail. The crest of the female is significantly lower, highest at the nape, and represented on the back usually by low, serrate scales. Coloration of males is brownish, greenish, or reddish, with or without dark netting. The outer edge of the eyelids is orange red, and the eyes are bright blue. The pale orange to reddish gular pouch has dark lines. Females have similar colors, but with different nuances; the back often has short yellow cross-bars and the sides have dark netting. The gular pouch is pale with dark longitudinal lines; the eyes are blue. Juveniles have the same coloration as adult females, but their eyes are brown; they also have bright green with reddish brown vertical bars on the head, back, legs, and tail. Three eggs (11 x 23 mm) are laid and at 20 to 24°C (68 to 75°F) they hatch after an incubation period of 97 days. These angleheads are found on tree trunks near water or somewhat farther away. Malaysian Peninsula, Borneo, Sumatra, Natuna Islands.
Literature: Manthey & Denzer, 1992b.

Gonocephalus robinsoni (Boulenger, 1908)

Notes: HBL male 115-152, female 115-132; TL male 285-320, female 290-300 mm. The sexes are hard to tell apart, but males have a thicker base of the tail. Both sexes have a continuous dorsal crest of triangular scales pointing slightly to the rear, the height decreasing regularly to the tail. The gular pouch is large for the genus and reaches to the breast. Both sexes are greenish olive, sometimes with dark diagonal vertical banding. Juveniles may have intense changes in colors, including light olive, green, or light brownish with dark vertical bars; there are contrasting head markings, and the legs and tail are cross-banded. Five to eight eggs (10 x 22 mm) are laid. Like other angleheads, it is found in montane forest not below 1000 meters, near flowing water on thin trees and

also on ferns along paths. Provide a cloud-forest terrarium. Malaysian Peninsula (Selangor and Pahang Provinces).
Literature: Manthey & Denzer, 1992a.

Harpesaurus Boulenger, 1885

Snout Agamas: 4 species
Characteristics: Like the horned agamas of Sri Lanka, the species in the genus *Harpesaurus* are equipped with hornlike snout appendages. They differ from the horned agamas through the visible tympanum and homogeneous, shingle-like dorsal scales. Gular pouches are not present in all species.
Habits: These chiefly arboreal agamids seem to prefer the same kinds of habitats as the species of the genus *Ceratophora*. The few known localities indicate that they inhabit montane rainforests.
Keeping: These agamids should initially be kept in larger cloud-forest terraria to determine the preferred temperature range. If necessary, the terrarium should be maintained at a slightly different temperature. Insects and worms should be offered as food.
Range: Nias Island, Sumatra, and Java.

Harpesaurus beccari Doria, 1888

Description: HBL 65-86, TL 140-164 mm. A forked horn 8 to 10 mm long on the tip of the snout distinguishes males from females. Nape, dorsal, and tail crests (on the first third of the tail) are clearly separated from one another in males; in females they are continuous. The back of the male is dominated by a bright green color that exhibits a bluish tinge or can tend to olive. The sides of the head, the shoulders, and the front sides of the upper front legs have short white bands.
Notes: At room temperature in the terrarium a male moved about as slowly as a chameleon. He stayed primarily on thin branches and fed on crawling and flying insects.
Range: About 1500 meters, western Sumatra.
Literature: Boehme, 1989; Manthey, 1990.

Harpesaurus modigliani Vinciguerra, 1933

Notes: HBL 83, TL 139 mm. A single horn

The male snout agama *Harpesaurus beccari* may be one of the most unusual-appearing agamids. Known only from Sumatra, it seldom has been kept by hobbyists. Photo: U. Manthey.

6 mm long is present on the snout. The nape crest is higher and separated from the dorsal crest, which is continuous to the middle of the tail and comprised of triangular scales; a gular pouch is present. Specimens are blue and green, with dark zones on the nape and the front part of the flanks. Found at about 1200 meters in the Si-Rambe Forest, northern Sumatra.

Harpesaurus tricinctus (A. Dumeril, 1851)

Notes: HBL 64, TL 83 mm. A single horn 21 mm long is present on the snout. A crest of triangular scales extends from the nape to the end of the tail without interruption. The lizard is dark in color with three conspicuous broad, light, vertical bands. Java.

Hydrosaurus Kaup, 1827

Sailfin Dragons: 2 to 4 species

Characteristics: Sailfins, with a total length of more than 1 meter (40 in), of which two-thirds is the tail, are the giants among the agamids. They have powerful legs with lobelike edges of skin on the fingers and toes as well as a laterally strongly flattened tail. A visible tympanum, a frontal crest, nape and dorsal crests, as well as femoral pores are present. The back is covered with keeled roof-tilelike scales, among which are scattered larger round ones. Adult males have a taller dermal crest on the tail than do females. The sexes of juveniles cannot be distinguished externally.

Comment: The taxonomic status of the species is uncertain. Some sailfins from the Philippines (*Hydrosaurus pustulatus*) exhibit enlarged scales above the tympanum that merge into a row of even larger, conical scales. The type specimen from the island of Ambon that was used to describe *Hydrosaurus amboinensis* displays a similar row. On the other hand, some specimens from New Guinea that were examined display two such rows. These populations, however, also are classified as *Hydrosaurus amboinensis*. Krasula (1988) illustrated a sexually mature male *Hydrosaurus pustulatus* with red eyes, while in a documented photograph of an adult Philippine male blue eyes are discernible. The differing length measurements and the remaining expression of the caudal crest appear to be more age-dependent and individually variable than species specific. The same is true of the frontal crest and the enlarged scales on the flanks.

Habits: Sailfins live exclusively in riparian (water-edge) zones with thick vegetation near diverse bodies of water that have enough water to dive into even in the dry season. They lie motionless for hours on overhanging branches with their legs hanging down limply. They rely on their camouflage up to a flight distance of 2 to 3 meters (80 to 120 in). If the lizards are frightened by hasty movements, however, they fall into the water, swim a few meters, and then disappear into the tangle of shoreline vegetation. Very young sailfins have been observed so far only on the ground. They quickly find hiding places under rocks and fallen leaves, as well as between roots, which they seek out at the slightest danger. A territory consisting of a few trees and bushes is occupied by male,

The Common Sailfin Dragon, *Hydrosaurus amboinensis*, is a large but interesting agamid that requires special care to keep successfully. Photo: H. Bielfeld.

several females, and the juveniles. They are very site-faithful. Animals in the wild feed almost exclusively on plants and sweet fruits, juveniles more on seeds. The eggs are buried 20 to 30 cm (8 to 12 in) deep in warm riparian sand.

Keeping: The care of these largest representatives of the agamids is problematic and very time-consuming. An unplanted rainforest terrarium (H abt. 200, L abt. 200, D abt. 130 cm) with an aquatic section 50 to 60 cm (20 to 30 in) covering about half the ground space is necessary. As a substrate, fine sieved gravel heated by a heating cable has proved effective. Each sailfin needs at least one diagonal climbing branch for itself alone. Wild-caught specimens need lots of quiet during the acclimation period and not infrequently refuse to eat. Hasty movements must always be avoided; a vi-

A group of sailfins feeding. Notice the large tail crest of the male in the background compared to the females in the foreground. Photo: M. Schmidt.

sual barrier can be helpful. Forced feeding subjects the agamids to too much stress, often with fatal results. Medium-sized animals, with a total length of 50 to 70 cm (20 to 28 in), more readily become acclimated to terrarium life than do juveniles, which are far more susceptible to stress. Although acclimated sailfins feed mostly on vegetable foods, they also take fish, chicks, mice, and insects. However, it must not be overlooked that in the wild they are almost exclusively herbivorous. Brightly colored fruits (yellow, orange, red) are preferred, but lettuce and young fig, mulberry, and willow leaves also are taken. Sailfins must be fed four to six times a day and must be given calcium and vitamin preparations at least once a week. If, despite all of these problems, you want to keep and breed sailfins, you must make sure that all the animals in one colony come from the same region. Only in this way can it be ensured that the group will be made up of the same species.

Range: Indo-Australasian Archipelago, including the Philippines and New Guinea.
Literature: Gaulke, 1989; Kopstein, 19xx; Krasula, 1988; Visser, 1984.

An adult male Common Sailfin, *Hydrosaurus amboinensis*. Photo: R. Heselhaus.

A juvenile Philippine Sailfin Dragon, *Hydrosaurus pustulatus*. The species of *Hydrosaurus* are very difficult to distinguish without locality data. Photo: R. D. Bartlett.

A young Philippine Sailfin Dragon, *Hydrosaurus pustulatus*, has a short and rounded snout. It looks quite different from the adult male. Photo: Grossmann.

In the adult male *Hydrosaurus pustulatus* the snout is strongly swollen, there are pointed "eyebrows," and the large scales on the side of the neck are especially heavy. Photo: Grossmann.

Hydrosaurus amboinensis (Schlosser, 1768)

Description: Because of the difficulty of classifying the species and the open taxonomic questions, descriptions of the individual species will not be given.

Reproduction: Four to six clutches of three to nine eggs are laid during a year, the dimensions of which are 18.5-27.1 x 38-46 mm. At 30°C (86°F) they require 60 to 73 days to develop. During the incubation period they reach a size of 44 x 63 mm.

Range: Indo-Australasian Archipelago including New Guinea.

Hydrosaurus pustulatus (Eschscholtz, 1829)

Reproduction: Two to five times a year, females lay four to ten eggs with dimen-

sions of 15 x 25 mm. During the approximately 70-day incubation period at 28.5 to 31°C (83 to 88°F) they grow to 38 x 68 mm. Newly hatched young have a total length of 210 to 240 mm.

Range: Philippines.

Hylagama Mertens, 1924

1 species

Characteristics: No external differences compared to the genus *Harpesaurus* are present.

Habits: The localities seem to show that this agamid is an inhabitant of the lowland rainforest. It is highly likely that *Hylagama borneensis* is found on trees and shrubs.

Keeping: A planted rainforest terrarium would seem to be suited for keeping. It is highly probable that *Hylagama* feeds on insects, but worms should be offered as well.

Range: Borneo.

More and more captive-bred sailfins (such as this young *Hydrosaurus pustulatus*) are available to hobbyists, but most specimens seen still are wild-caught. Photo: R. D. Bartlett.

Adults of the Common Sailfin, *Hydrosaurus amboinensis*, often exceed a meter in length and require a sufficiently large terrarium with a large pond or tank of water. Their care may be beyond the capability of the average hobbyist. Photo: P. Freed.

Hylagama borneensis Mertens, 1924

Description: HBL male 52, female 55-59; TL male 97, female 87-93 mm. Small triangular scales, separated by an interval of one dorsal scale, make up the nape and dorsal crest of both sexes. The dorsal crest of the male ends on the tail; in the female it is lower and ends before the tail. On the tip of the snout of the male is a cylindrical horn 7 mm long. In the same place in the female there is only a bump approximately 1.5 mm high. The back of the female displays black speckling on an olive-green base. Diagonal orange cross-bars adorn the sides, and large brown specks cover the middle of the back from the nape to the lumbar region. The pinkish orange labial scales stand out from the dark gray of the throat and the gular pouch. The belly is whitish.

Reproduction: Two eggs about 10 mm long are laid.

Range: Central and western Kalimantan (apparently on the Kapuas River); at Hiah and Nanga Tekalit, Kapit District, on the Mengiong River, both localities on Sarawak.

Literature: King, 1978.

An adult Common Sailfin Dragon, *Hydrosaurus amboinensis*. Photo: P. Freed.

Notice the gigantic feet of this adult Philippine Sailfin, *Hydrosaurus pustulatus.* Obviously such a large, specialized lizard cannot be kept in a 400-liter terrarium. Photo: A. Norman.

The forest dragon *Hypsilurus dilophus* is found on many islands around New Guinea. Photo: U. Manthey.

Hypsilurus Peters, 1867

Forest Dragons: 13 species

Characteristics: Until recently *Hypsilurus* was considered to be a synonym of *Gonocephalus*, and it apparently is not externally distinguishable from the angleheads. All species have nape and dorsal crests, visible tympana, and strongly keeled ventral scales.

Habits: As far as is known, forest dragons are found in similar habitats to the angleheads and live on rainforest trees of the lowlands and uplands.

Keeping: See the genus *Gonocephalus*.

Range: New Guinea and surrounding islands; Micronesia; Melanesia; Australia.

Hypsilurus spinipes (A. Dumeril, 1851)

Southern Forest Dragon

Description: HBL male 105-113, female 103-110; TL male 220-250, female 215-220 mm; hatchlings 33-34 + 50-52 mm (HBL + TL). On the curved nape crest, which resembles a lobe of skin, there are triangular crest scales. The separate dorsal crest exhibits the same kind of scales and ends on the tail. Between the small dorsal scales are scattered numerous larger scales. Both sexes

have a plain light brownish gray ground color with indistinct dark markings. Radiating dark stripes above the eye as well as dark vertical lines on the lips are exhibited only by females and juveniles.

The female *Hypsilurus spinipes*, the Southern Forest Dragon, lacks the exaggerated crest of the male. Photo: Manning.

Habitat and behavior: *Hypsilurus spinipes* inhabits rainforests and other moist woodlands, in which males establish territories of 300-700 square meters. Between the adjoining territories of the individual males there are corridors 1 to 6 meters (3.3 to 20 ft) wide that they usually avoid. Through field experiments it was demonstrated that male intruders are driven off by biting and chasing. Females also seem to establish territories. The tendency to move is quite variable. On some days males walk or climb distances of only 2 to 3 meters (6.6 to 10 ft); on others, in contrast, they move up to 80 meters (264 ft). Most of the movement takes place on the ground (58-74 percent). Climbing plants and young trees with an average diameter of 2 to 6 cm (1 to 2.5 in) are a favorite habit of the agamids. Their body temperature is usually somewhat higher than that of the environment. The activity phase is in a temperature range of 15.5 to 25.1°C (60 to 77°F). At dusk they seek out roosting places at heights of 1 to 8 meters (3.3 to 27 ft).

Reproduction: In the breeding season the males are quite aggressive toward one another. Between October and January, during the first strong rains after a long dry period, the females begin to search for a suitable place to lay their eggs. This spot must be exposed to direct sunlight in the afternoon. Because such places are rare in thick forests, they are occasionally visited by several females. They excavate several shallow, triangular test nests. In several stages the clutch is either laid in a nest and covered sparsely with soil or deposited on a layer of leaves. (This behavior was observed in the wild; however, the female was disturbed by various circumstances.) The two to seven eggs (13 x 22 mm) per clutch develop within 74 days at an average temperature of 17.5 to 19.2°C (64 to 66°F). The embryos need about six hours to escape from the egg. Every two hours they remove a little of the egg membrane for periods of 10 to 15 minutes. After hatching the youngsters lie beside the egg with stiff bodies and closed eyes and play dead. They maintain this posture even when they are picked up.

Range: Altitudes of 50-1110 meters, isolated areas of the Great Dividing Range on the eastern coast of Australia, between Gyhmpie in the north and Gosford in the south.

Literature: Manning & Ehmann, 1991; Manning, 1991.

Hypsilurus dilophus (Dumeril & Bibron, 1837)

Notes: HBL male 152-213, female 165-188; TL male 255-357, female 255-320 mm. High, wide lanceolate crest scales are present on the nape; the dorsal crest is separate and is made up of similar scales continuing to the tip of the tail. Another crest of triangular scales is present on the forward edge of the huge gular pouch. Smaller scales on the back are mixed with larger ones throughout, including on the gular pouch. Males have a thickened base of the tail. Coloration is variable, the body greenish black to yellowish brown, the head more yellowish; the male has a red iris and eye ring. The species is closely tied to water and needs a rainforest terrarium. Two eggs are laid. Aru and Kai Islands, Batana, New Guinea, Ferguson Island, and D'Entrecasteaux Islands.

Hypsilurus godeffroyi Peters, 1867

Notes: HBL male 114-160, female 90-120; TL male 323-547, female 275-440 mm. From the occiput to the first third of the tail there is a continuous dorsal crest of lanceolate to triangular scales on a fold of skin from the nape over the back. All body scales are keeled, and the dorsal scales are smaller than the ventral scales. Both sexes have a gular pouch. Males are gray-green to gray-brown, the rear third of body and beginning of the tail often mauve; the gular pouch is cream to light or dark gray, often with round yellow, orange, and black specks. Females have the back uniformly gray, the sides in part speckled with black, and the belly yellow or yellow green. Juveniles and females are basically green, but males have dark vertical bands. It is a rainforest dweller found on trunks and branches. Insects are the basic food, but rarely small lizards are taken along with fruits and other

A large forest dragon, *Hypsilurus* sp. (near *godeffroyi*) from New Guinea. Photo: K. H. Switak.

An Australian Forest Dragon, *Hypsilurus spinipes*, from Narama, Australia. Photo: R. W. Van Devender.

Hypsilurus sp. (near *godeffroyi*) from New Guinea. Photo: K. H. Switak.

Japalura splendida, a mountain agama from western China. Photo: U. Manthey.

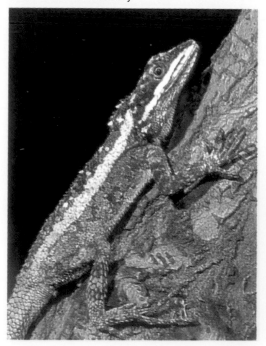

plants. Two or three eggs are laid; they mature in six to eight weeks. New Guinea, Caroline and Solomon Islands.
Literature: McCoy, 1980.

Japalura Gray, 1853

Mountain Agamas: 24 species and at least 3 subspecies

Characteristics: These predominantly small agamids share definitive generic characteristics. The genus seems to be in need of revision, and the species are difficult to tell apart. The body is more or less laterally flattened and provided with irregularly arranged scales of unequal size on the back. Several species have nape and dorsal crests as well as gular pouches, others do not. The tympanum is visible or concealed.

Habits: Virtually nothing is known of the habits of the individual species. Several species seem to live exclusively terrestrially in grassy or rocky landscapes, while others appear to be more or less arboreal.

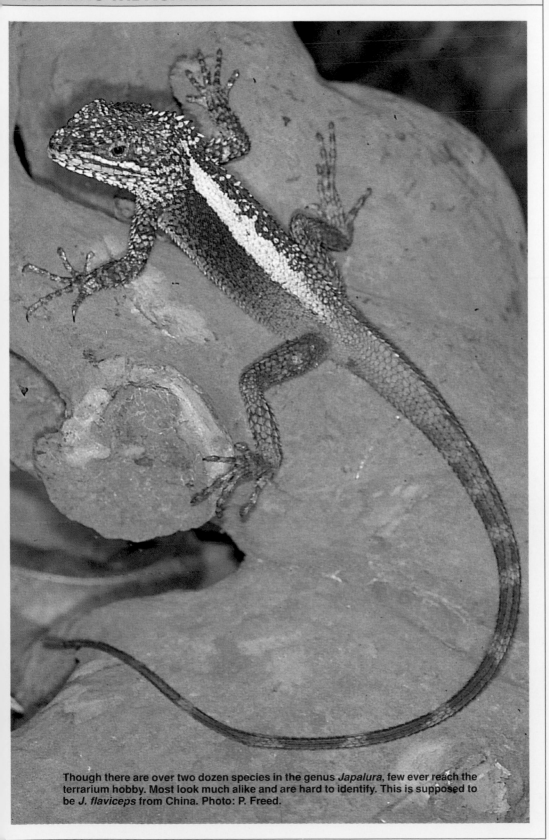

Though there are over two dozen species in the genus *Japalura*, few ever reach the terrarium hobby. Most look much alike and are hard to identify. This is supposed to be *J. flaviceps* from China. Photo: P. Freed.

Keeping: General recommendations are impossible. It can be assumed that all species feed on insects, but some may also be specialized to feed on ants. These small agamids mostly come from mountainous regions, where the temperature falls substantially at night.

Range: Up to about 3000 meters. Himalaya region, Burma, northern Thailand (?), Cambodia, Laos (?), Vietnam, southern China, Taiwan (main island as well as Lanyu and Lutao Islands), Japan (Ryukyu Islands).

Literature: Smith, 1935; Ota, 1991.

Japalura major (Jerdon, 1870)

Notes: HBL male 85; TL male 155 mm, female smaller. The body is slightly flattened laterally. The nape and dorsal crests of very small triangular scales, continuing to the tail. The occiput has a variable number and arrangement of spiny scales. The dorsal scales are variable in form and size, but usually there are large, keeled, roof-tilelike scales, often in longitudinal rows. The back is olive to green with V-shaped markings. This is a terrestrial species that is very sluggish and lives on rocks or in grass. Females lay ten eggs (8-8.5 x 13-14.5 mm) in June. Up to 2500 meters, western Himalayas.

Literature: Jamdar, 1985.

Japalura polygonata polygonata Hallowell, 1861

Notes: HBL male 75, female 65; TL male 150, female 130 mm. A small nape crest is present, and the dorsal crest is suggested through flat, identical scales. Small spines are on the end of the curve of the eyebrow, above and behind the tympanum. The small dorsal scales are mixed with numerous larger scales. Males are green with a diagonal light stripe from the tympanum to the belly just in front of the hind legs; females are dark green with five brown vertical bars. Found on trees and on the ground, it is a forest species and a follower of civilization. Provide a rainforest terrarium (H abt. 100, L abt. 80, D abt. 50 cm). An insectivore that is fond of wax moths, it is an unproblematic captive. One to four eggs are laid in the summer. Amami and Okinawa Islands. *Japalura polygonata ishigakiensis* —Japan (Miyako and Yaeyama Islands); *Japalura polygonata xanthostoma*—lowlands of northern Taiwan.

Literature: Sengoku, 1979; Stejneger, 1907.

Japalura splendida Barbour & Dunn, 1919

Notes: HBL male 80-92, male 72; TL male 185-217, female 176 mm. The body

Recently a few *Japalura*, such as this *J. splendida*, have entered the market from China and Vietnam. Photo: R. D. Bartlett.

Many species of *Japalura* are poorly known to Western hobbyists. This is a female *J. nepalensis*, a species almost unknown in captivity. Photo: R. G. Sprackland.

is dorsolaterally flattened, the head dorsoventrally flattened (longer and broader in male). The tympanum is concealed and there is a small gular pouch. There is a tubercular scale on each side of the occiput. The dorsal scales are small, rooftilelike, keeled, and mixed with larger scales of the same kind. There is a low nape crest of triangular scales, and the dorsal crest is suggested. The base of the tail is thickened and elongated in both sexes. The head is black above with turquoise markings or vertical bars. The upper labials have light and dark areas, and above them is a whitish stripe from the tip of the snout to the corner of the mouth. There is a black band above the eye, continuing with interruptions on the flanks. Light dorsolateral bands (yellow, green, or olive) extend from the occiput to the tail between a broad dark vertebral band with turquoise spots or vertical stripes. The extremities often are green. The belly is light olive, the tip of the gular pouch greenish. However, lizards may be entirely black. An upland species, it probably lives on trees or rocks. It is an insectivore. A warmth-loving species, females are shyer than males. Provide a dry-forest or cloud-forest terrarium; over-wintering apparently is necessary. Altitudes of 100 to about 3000 meters, Szechuan and Yunnan (?), western China. **Literature:** Pope, 1935.

Laudakia Gray, 1845
Whorl-tail Agamas: approximately 22 species and 11 subspecies

Characteristics: These medium-sized agamids have a dorsoventrally flattened body, often with lateral folds of skin. The tail is covered with whorls or rings of scales. A dorsal crest is absent. The flat, triangular head, which lacks a gular pouch, exhibits a large tympanum and a gular fold, which usually merges into the shoulder fold. Males usually exhibit thickened ventral and preanal scales.

Habits: When danger threatens, cliff-dwelling *Laudakia* species flee like a flash from their observation posts into narrow crevices and wedge themselves in by inflating the body. Arboreal species hide in holes in the ground, under loose bark, or move to the opposite side of the tree trunk. Although these agamids in part

A head study of *Japalura splendida*. Photo: R. D. Bartlett.

The Blue-throated or Tree Agama, *Laudakia atricollis*, is a familiar agamid of dry eastern Africa. Photo: K. H. Switak.

maintain a large flight distance, several inhabit house walls and stone walls. Though some species are solitary, others display a permanent social structure with a dominant male, several females, and lower-ranking males. *Laudakia* species from the northern part of the range hibernate, whereas tropical species may estivate in the dry season. They feed on insects, smaller lizards, and plants.

Keeping: See *Agama.* The temperature should be 25 to 40°C (77 to 104°F) during the day; a distinct cooling at night is necessary. *Laudakia* species can be kept outside in the summer. Because they are sensitive to persistent wetness combined with low temperatures, protection from rain and a place to warm up are absolutely necessary. It has proved beneficial to always cover half of the outdoor cage with UV-permeable plexiglass. Northern populations must hibernate. Wild-caught specimens lose little of their shyness in the terrarium, but juveniles and captive-bred specimens become more trusting.

Range: From extreme southeastern Europe through southwestern Asia to central Asia and Mongolia, also parts of the Arabian Peninsula across the Sinai to northeastern Africa, and East Africa to southern Africa.

Laudakia adramitana (Anderson, 1896)

Yemeni Blue Agama

Description: HBL male 148, female 118; TL male 222, female 177 mm; hatchlings 45 mm total length. The tail whorls are only weakly expressed. The back is covered with small granulated scales, but larger keeled scales are present on the legs. The yellowish ground color is covered with an irregular pattern of broad, dark netting. At high temperatures and in the breeding season, males exhibit their brightest deep blue coloration. The sulfur-yellow front part of the tail stands in contrast to the coloration of the rest of the body. In females only the head turns blue.

Habitat and behavior: These terrestrial agamids establish their territories in arid rocky regions.

Reproduction: After the rare, brief rainfalls, females bury four to six eggs in the ground. In the terrarium, the initially somewhat delicate youngsters hatch after two to three months.

A colorful male Yemeni Blue Agama, *Laudakia adramitana*, in breeding color. Photo: Zernikow.

Notes: An ideal breeding group consists of one male and two females; several males may not be kept together. Although *Laudakia adramitana* does not hibernate in its homeland, a four-week drop in temperature and reduction in light has a positive effect on the breeding condition.

Range: Yemen.

Laudakia atricollis atricollis (Smith, 1849)
Blue-throated Agama
Description: HBL male 145, female 141; TL male 194, female 175 mm; hatchlings 55-60 mm in total length. The slightly keeled dorsal scales are mixed with small, cream-colored spiny scales. The male has a conspicuously large eye and cheek tuberosities on the broad, massive head. Their back is brownish or light greenish with a dark shoulder patch. When excited the head, throat, front legs, front part of the body, flanks, and the tip of the tail turn bright blue. In the female a blackish brown rhomboid pattern runs along the side of the medium-gray back.

Habitat and behavior: These agamids live in wooded savannahs and open forests primarily on trees, but can also be found on rock piles.

Reproduction: In courtship the males assume their brightest colors. They raise the tail vertically and carry out wriggling movements with the tip. In March and April three to eight eggs are laid, from which the youngsters hatch in two to three months. Their rearing is problematic only in the first days. After that they can be kept together with the parents, since the species does not tend to cannibalism.

Notes: If wasps are fed, the lizards lose all shyness and hunt them in their brightest colors.

Range: *Laudakia atricollis gregori*—coastal strip in Kenya; *Laudakia atricollis kuwuensis*—Congo; *Laudakia atricollis loveridgei*—Tanzania; *Laudakia atricollis minuta*—Ethiopia, Kenya; *Laudakia atricollis ugandaensis*—Uganda, Tanzania.

Laudakia caucasia (Eichwald, 1831)
Caucasus Mountain Agama
Description: HBL male up to 150; TL up to 200 mm, female slightly smaller; hatchlings 35-43 mm HBL. *Laudakia caucasia* has a relatively narrow and flat head as well as a dorsoventrally strongly flattened body. In contrast to *Laudakia stellio*, it has smooth throat scales and uniform dorsal scales on the central part

of the back. The olive-gray to sand-colored, blackish brown, or reddish back has an irregular dark netting that includes small light specks. In the breeding season the throat, breast, and flanks of the male take on an almost black color. They are easy to recognize by the always paler ventral patch.

Habitat and behavior: Caucasus Mountain Agamas live in mountainous regions at altitudes between 300 and 3370 meters on dry, hot rocky slopes and scree with sparse vegetation. When danger threatens they retreat into crevices or other hollow spaces. By inflating the body they become wedged in their hiding place. A male together with one to three females occupy a territory. From November to March many agamids assemble in especially favorable sites, where they overwinter together. The diet consists chiefly of insects and smaller amounts of leaves, flowers, and berries.

Reproduction: After mating between March and June, starting in May the female lays 4 to 14 eggs (average size 13 x 23 mm) up to twice a year. At incubation temperatures of 28 to 34°C (82 to 94°F) during the day and 25 to 26°C (77 to 79°F) at night, the youngsters appear after 63 to 72 days. At higher temperatures (34°C [94°F] day, 28°C [82°F] night), almost exclusively males hatch. Rearing is difficult.

Notes: Before laying their eggs, females behave very aggressively. The small number of suitable laying sites in some regions can even lead to fighting between them. They often guard and defend their clutch. In captivity, this species can live more than 17 years.

Range: From Dagestan, Transcaucusus, southern Turkmen across northeastern Turkey to Iraq, Iran, Afghanistan, and Pakistan.
Literature: Wegner, 1990.

Laudakia stellio (Linnaeus, 1758)
Hardun Agama
Description: HBL male 148, TL 200 mm; hatchlings 35 mm HBL. The small roof-tilelike dorsal scales are arranged in vertical rows and broken up by larger tubercular scales. The very dark back is covered with fairly large dark yellow patches that are reduced to spots on the flanks. The tail is banded in yellow and black. In contrast to the dark gray ventral side of the female, the belly and throat of the male are deep black. The front legs of the male turn dark blue in the breeding season.

Habitat and behavior: These terrestrial agamids inhabit stone walls and rocks of the plains. At low population densities the animals often live in pairs; otherwise they form larger groups.

Reproduction: Mating occurs between March and early June. Starting in May, three clutches (in the terrarium up to five) of three to eight eggs (average 11 x 19 mm) are laid and buried. The incubation period is 52 to 55 days.

Notes: In the terrarium *Laudakia stellio picea* withdraws in the winter into its hiding place, which it leaves only occasionally to drink. Food is not taken. After two months at reduced temperature and lighting, the agamid again displays a lively

There are many described subspecies of the Hardun, *Laudakia stellio*. This is *L. s. picea* from the northern Middle East. Photo: W. Schmidt.

behavior and is ready to breed. It is one of the few species that becomes "finger tame" after a short acclimation period. Only one male can be kept together with a maximum of five females.

Range: *Laudakia stellio brachydactyla*—northern Saudi Arabia, southern Israel, and the Sinai, southern Jordan; *Laudakia stellio cypriacus*—Cyprus; *Laudakia stellio daani*—Salonika and numerous islands in the Aegean Sea, Asia Minor to Israel; *Laudakia stellio picea*—southwestern Syria, southern Lebanon, northern Israel, northwestern Jordan; *Laudakia stellio stellio*—Mykonos Island; *Laudakia stellio vulgaris*—northern Egypt.

Literature: Beutler, 1981.

Leiolepis Cuvier, 1829

Butterfly Agamas: 4 species and 4 subspecies

Characteristics: *Leiolepis* is closely related to *Uromastyx*, and both genera together are considered by some authors to make up their own subfamily or even an independent family (Leiolepidinae). The body is more strongly flattened dorsoventrally than is the more rounded tail. The back is covered with very small, granular, homogeneous scales. The tympanum is visible. Femoral pores are present in both sexes; on the other hand, a gular pouch and nuchal and dorsal crests are totally absent.

Habits: No other agamids in Southeast Asia are as specialized for life above and under the ground as the butterfly agamas. They prefer open, more arid areas with sandy soils. There they dig burrows about 30 cm (12 in) deep and up to 70 cm (28 in) long that serve as living and hiding places. The predominantly monogamous lizards live in groups, but inhabit their burrows alone or in pairs together with the young of the year. Because they definitely need a lot of warmth, they leave their shelter only in sunny weather during the warmest hours of the day. At a temperature of 33°C (91°F) in the shade, the ground in

A head study of the Hardun, *Laudakia stellio brachydactyla*, a form sometimes imported from the Sinai. Photo: W. P. Mara.

Laudakia lehmani is a seldom-seen agama from Afghanistan and central Asia. Photo: P. Freed.

the sun is heated to about 53°C (135°F), and the agamids display their full activity. At these times they can run at tremendous speeds. Their greatly elongated, free-ended ribs permit an extreme flattening of the body, which serves for greater warmth collection and simultaneously enables them to wedge themselves into the burrow. In addition, this reputedly enables them to make gliding jumps of 10 to 12 meters (33 to 40 ft). Under laboratory conditions, however, only shorter distances of one to barely two meters (3.3 to 6.6 ft) could be documented. In their range the *Leiolepis* species are the only agamids that are regularly offered on the market as food. To prevent them from escaping, their backbones and legs are broken or several are closely bundled and tied together. In the weekend market in Bangkok, they are sold skinned on ice.

Many Common Butterfly Agamas, *Leiolepis b. belliana*, that live along the coast feed on small crustaceans as well as insects and plants. Photo: U. Manthey.

Keeping: *Leiolepis* species are primarily vegetarian but do not spurn insects. To offer them the necessary room in which to move, an arid terrarium must have a width of at least 3 meters (10 ft) and a depth of more than 70 cm (28 in). The substrate should be 30 to 50 cm (12 to 20 in) deep and consist of a mixture of sand and loam. The agamids must be able to excavate their holes and passages without danger of collapse. A part of the terrarium must be kept somewhat cooler (25 to 33°C, 77 to 91°F) and damper; in contrast, temperatures of 45 to 50°C (115 to 130°F) are necessary at the basking spot. Room temperature is sufficient at night. The animals are well suited for outdoor-keeping in the summer. Because they do not tolerate cool dampness, a partial covering of the terrarium with UV-permeable double-pane plexiglass is useful. When nights are too cold, everything must be covered.

Range: Burma east to southern China and the island of Hainan, south to Sumatra and the island of Bangka.

Literature: Peters, 1971.

Leiolepis belliana belliana **(Gray, 1827)**

Common Butterfly Agama

Description: HBL male 103-156, female 107-145; TL male up to 300, female up to 280 mm. The nominate form is easily recognized by the three yellow, dark-bordered dorsal stripes on a light brown ground color. Between the usually very even, narrow stripes containing rounded specks run one or two longitudinal rows of separate yellowish ocelli. In juveniles these ocelli fuse into stripes and the tail is bright red. Both sexes exhibit black flanks from which seven to nine orange-red vertical bars stand out in contrast. The legs and tail have light speckling on the dorsal side.

Notes: Because the lizards inhabit tracts of land near the coast in the tropics, the terrarium must have a high humidity during the day. These agamids are peaceful toward other terrarium inhabitants and become very confiding after a while. They prefer insects to vegetable food, which is only taken occasionally. In their

The colorful alternating bars of black and orange are a trademark of the Common Butterfly Agama, *Leiolepis belliana*. Photo: G. Dingerkus.

Leiolepis reevesi often is called the Northern Butterfly Agama. Notice that the black bars are restricted to the arm insertion. Photo: P. Freed.

natural habitat they also feed on small crabs.

Range: Northeastern coast of the Gulf of Thailand between the Menam and Mekong Deltas; coastal region of the Thai/Malaysian Peninsula, as well as a few nearby islands; coastal strip of Sumatra and Bangka Island.

Leiolepis belliana ocellata Peters, 1971

Notes: The flanks are black with light vertical bands. The back is thickly covered with light oval ocelli whose dark edgings can form vertical bars. The re-

maining outer longitudinal stripes usually are retained in adults in the pelvic region. Burma and mountainous regions of northern Thailand.

Lophocalotes Guenther, 1872

1 species

Characteristics: In contrast to all other arboreal agamids, *Lophocalotes* exhibits smooth scale lamellae under the fingers and toes. Their massive-looking head has a visible tympanum, but no gular pouch. The entire body is covered with large shingle-like scales.

Range: Western Sumatra.

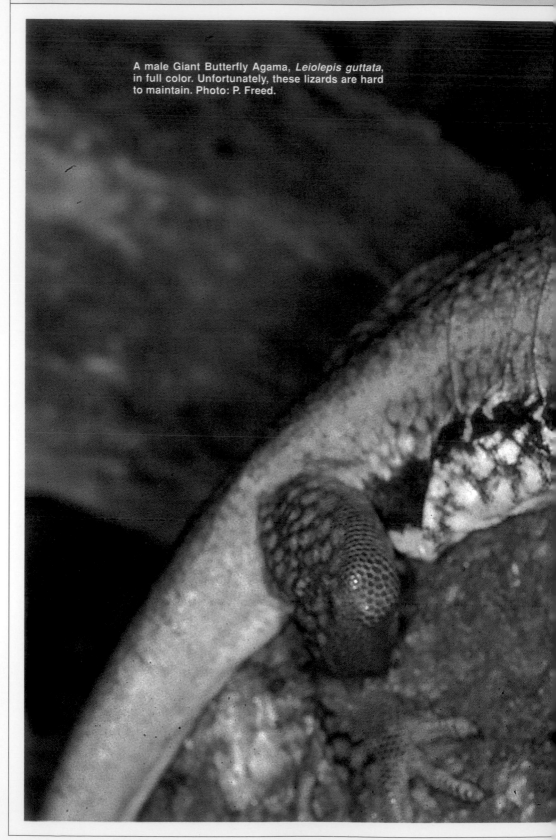

A male Giant Butterfly Agama, *Leiolepis guttata*, in full color. Unfortunately, these lizards are hard to maintain. Photo: P. Freed.

Top: An adult male Northern Crested Dragon, *Lophognathus [Amphibolurus] temporalis*, photographed in Kakadu National Park, Northern Territory, Australia. This genus is very closely related to *Amphibolurus* and often considered a synonym. Photo: K. H. Switak. Bottom: A rather colorless female *Lophognathus [Amphibolurus] gilberti* from Queensland, Australia. Photo: R. W. Van Devender.

On look-out! A male Northern Crested Dragon, *Lophognathus [Amphibolurus] temporalis*. Photo: K. H. Switak.

Lophocalotes ludekingi (Bleeker, 1860)

Notes: HBL 88-92, TL 140-152 mm. The nape crest consists of sharp, lanceolate scales; the separate dorsal crest comprises similar scales pointing slightly to the rear. The dorsal scales are irregular in size, not identical or aligned regularly, and some are keeled. The cheeks and the base of the tail of males are strongly thickened. The back is green, light turquoise toward the belly, with whitish specks or vertical bands; the throat and ventral side are light blue. Provide a cloud-forest terrarium for this insectivore. Altitudes of 1400-2800 meters, Mount Singalang and Alahanpanjang, Sumatra.

Lyriocephalus Merrem, 1820

Lyre-headed Agamas: 1 species

Characteristics: The conspicuously high, pointed curve of the eyebrows is also present in several angleheads. In contrast to them, however, a visible tympanum is absent in *Lyriocephalus*. In addition, adults have bulbous frontal appendages.

Habits: These odd agamas inhabit cool forests of the uplands, which in the meantime have become more open because of human disturbance. They stay on tree trunks. The males exhibit a pronounced territorial behavior and usually maintain a distance of 40 meters (132 ft) from one another. The agamids move slowly and when threatened often rely on their camouflage.

Keeping: Only a pair should be kept together in a planted rainforest terrarium (H abt. 140, L abt. 150, D abt. 60 cm). Lyreheads feed on insects but also show a special fondness for earthworms. They are peaceful terrarium inhabitants but are hard to keep and breed.

Range: Altitudes of 150-900 meters, central uplands of Sri Lanka.

Lyriocephalus scutatus (Linnaeus, 1758)

Lyre-headed Agama

Description: HBL male 127-170, TL 116-170 mm, female smaller; hatchlings 56-70 mm in total length. Both sexes have an erectile nape crest, which is taller in males. The continuous dorsal crest is made up of triangular scales that exhibit a clear separation and end on the tail. A mixture of small and large scales covers the dorsal side of the body. The coloration varies from dark brown through light brown to green. Adult males have a thickened base of the tail. They principally exhibit shades of green on the back, a bluish white ventral side, and a yellow gular pouch. When they are highly agitated the head, the nape crest, and part of the body turn yellow. Females also are greenish, but in the presence of a male they appear more gray-brown to brownish green. Juveniles exhibit a similar coloration. The inside of the mouth is a conspicuous red in all age groups.

Reproduction: Sexual maturity is reached after ten months. Under terrarium conditions two to five clutches are laid a year. The female lays 1 to 16 eggs (usually 8 to 12) that grow from an initial size of 12-23 x 18-22 to 20-22 x 30-31 mm. The incubation period is 141 to 151 days at 23 to 26°C (73 to 79°F).

Notes: Small rearing terraria and large groups of youngsters (four to eight individuals per enclosure) cause stress that only a few young survive.

Literature: Kiehlmann, 1980; Prinz & Prinz, 1986.

Mictopholis Smith, 1935

1 species

Characteristics: The body is laterally flattened and the back is covered with irregularly arranged scales that vary in size and form. The ventral scales also are of variable size. A gular pouch, tympanum, and nape crest (dorsal crest in the male?) are present.

Habits: No information is known. The laterally flattened body indicates that it is an arboreal species.

Keeping: Unfortunately, no descriptions of the habitat are known. Keeping specimens in a cloud-forest or rainforest terrarium would therefore have to be tried first. They probably feed on insects.

Range: Vicinity of Harmatti, Dafla Hills, Assam, India.

Mictopholis austeniana (Annandale, 1908)

Notes: HBL female 90, TL 230 mm. The

The very common Australian lizards formerly placed in *Amphibolurus* have been fragmented into several genera that are not recognized by all authors. *Lophognathus* (here the species *temporalis*) is considered by the author of this book to be a component of the basic genus *Amphibolurus*. Photo: K. H. Switak.

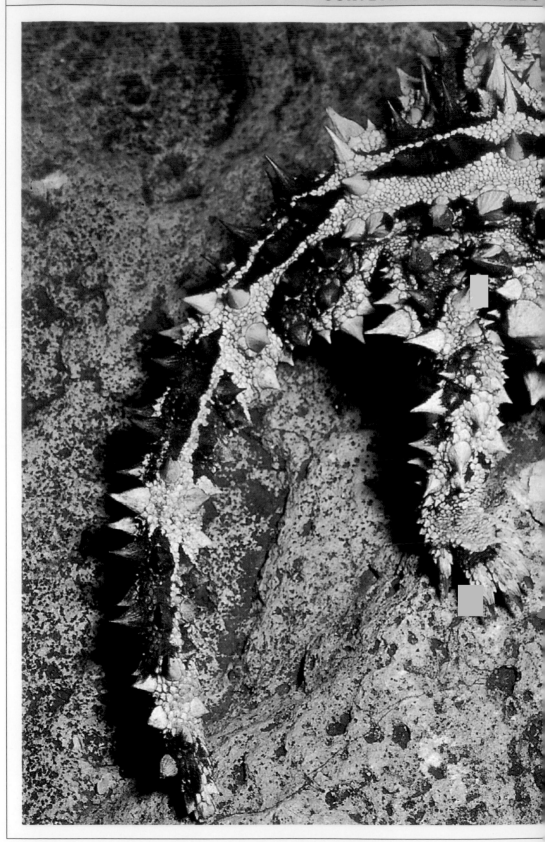

The Moloch or Thorny Devil, *Moloch horridus*, is an ant specialist and virtually impossible to keep alive in captivity outside Australia. The teeth project outward from the jaws rather than upward. Photo: K. Lucas.

nape crest is made of low, crescent-shaped scales pointing to the rear; the dorsal crest is suggested through a row of flattened scales. Dorsal and lateral scales are very irregular, small or large, keeled or smooth, rectangular or round. The lizard probably is predominantly various shades of green in life.

Moloch Gray, 1841
Thorny Devils
Characteristics: The entire dorsal side, including the extremities, the head, and the tail, exhibits large, relatively soft spines. On the nape is a large hump.

Moloch horridus. Photo: N. Schuster.

Habits: The Thorny Devil lives on sandy soils in arid to semi-arid, open grassy, bushy, and acacia-forested landscapes.

Keeping: This species should not be kept in captivity because they are dietary specialists on ants and usually refuse all other insects. Although newly hatched youngsters have been kept alive for more than a year with small Mediterranean crickets and mayflies, this experience does not seem to be worth repeating.

Range: Central, southern, and western Australia.

Moloch horridus Gray, 1841
Thorny Devil, Moloch
Description: HBL female 100, TL 90 mm, male somewhat smaller. The striking yellow, dark orange, to olive-gray or brownish pattern is interrupted by narrow light vertebral and dorsolateral stripes. From the nape to over the eye, spines extend in a Y-shaped pattern.

Habitat and behavior: This agamid, which is solitary outside the breeding season, travels over large areas but also temporarily stays in smaller areas. The tail is curved upward like a scorpion's when they run. Their movements are jerky, like a watch movement. As a result of the relatively long legs, the body can be raised well above the hot ground so that any contact is avoided. Molochs wait along ant trails and eat as many as 5000 ants at one sitting. The Moloch has an unusual way of taking up water. Porous scales between the spines have capillary-like pores that conduct the water to the corners of the mouth. The spines seem to be able to collect dew and to conduct the moisture to the capillaries. In defensive posture Thorny Devils raise their bodies and place the head between the front legs. They exhibit their greatest activity between March and May and from August to December. They can live to 20 years of age.

Reproduction: Sexual maturity is attained at about three years of age. During fights between rivals, the males ram their opponent much as do certain turtles. Females lay their three to ten eggs in long, diagonal burrows. The incubation period is 90 to 128 days.

Oriocalotes Guenther, 1864
1 species
Characteristics: The body is barely flattened laterally. The roof-tilelike dorsal scales of different sizes are regularly shaped and arranged. Nape and dorsal crests are present. The gular pouch and fold are absent, and the base of the tail of the male is not thickened. The tympanum often is concealed by scales.

Habits: Unknown, but perhaps similar to those of the *Calotes* species.

Keeping: Keeping this species in a cloud-forest terrarium may work. They probably eat insects.

Range: Khasi Hills, Assam, India; Sikkim?.

Oriocalotes paulus Smith, 1935
Notes: HBL male 48, female 70; TL male 95, female 130 mm. A nape crest of eight to ten low, separate spines is present, and there is a suggestion of a similar dorsal crest of even shorter spines. A

spine is present on the curve of the eyebrow and two others are above the tympanum. The dorsal scales are variable in size, keeled, and shingle-like. The lizard has extremely short legs. The male has a thickened, long base of tail. The color of living specimens is unknown. Five eggs are laid.

Otocryptis Wagler, 1830
Ground Agamas: 2 species
Characters: In the *Otocryptis* species the very long, thin legs are conspicuous. The laterally flattened body is covered on the back by variable-sized keeled scales. Males have a low nape crest. A gular pouch may be present or absent.
Range: Southern India and Sri Lanka.

Otocryptis wiegmanni Wagler, 1830
Sri Lankan Ground Agama
Description: HBL male 55-70, female 46-62; TL male 150-180, female 115-148 mm; hatchlings 15 + 40 mm (HBL + TL). This delicate agamid has a small head, a slender body, and a round tail. If the tail breaks off, it regenerates as a pear-shaped growth. The dorsal coloration exhibits various shades of gray-brown and can change into a pale reddish brown or olive-brown. The light dorsal band can take on the coloration of the flanks. It is sometimes edged by even lighter longitudinal stripes and exhibits dark vertical bands. The head and nape coloration is very variable. Males have a huge gular pouch reaching up to half of the body length. It is bright yellow-orange and has red V-shaped markings or a red patch. When the throat pouch is folded, two orange longitudinal stripes are visible on the breast.
Habitat and behavior: *Otocryptis wiegmanni* prefers shady and low branches of smaller trees and bushes along streams, in which it likes to bathe. Both sexes defend their territory against conspecifics. The threat behavior of the male includes the raising of the nape crest, nodding of the head, wriggling movements of the tail, and above all the rhythmic expansion of the gular pouch. The attacker springs on its opponent, which subsequently flees or presses itself flat to the ground in a type of submissive behav-

ior. The victor usually withdraws. If the fight also includes biting, however, serious mutual injuries can result. Females not in breeding condition exhibit the same submissive behavior; the head also turns black.
Keeping: Try a large, heavily planted rainforest terrarium (H abt. 120, L abt. 140, D abt. 60 cm) with thin branches. Only one pair may be kept per terrarium. The tastes of these insectivores vary greatly from individual to individual.
Reproduction: In the rainforest, matings occur throughout the year. The male courts while displaying his colorful head, raised nape crest, and constant nodding of the head. At monthly intervals

A male Sri Lankan Ground Agama, *Otocryptis wiegmanni*. Photo: U. Manthey.

three to seven, usually four, eggs (7-7.5 x 10-14 mm) are laid. During the incubation period of 51 to 70 days at an average temperature of 20 to 24°C (68 to 75°F), the eggs grow to about 11 x 17 mm.
Notes: The rearing terrarium must not be too small and must have adequate temperature gradients. Newly hatched youngsters prefer slower food animals at first.
Range: Sri Lanka, more commonly in the moist zone up to about 1000 meters than in the arid zone.
Literature: Manthey, 1985b.

Phoxophrys Hubrecht, 1881
5 species
Characteristics: The small *Phoxophrys* species have neither gular pouches nor frontal appendages. Dorsal and nape crests can be present or absent. Males

Portrait of *Phoxophrys nigrilabris* from Borneo. Photo: U. Manthey.

exhibit a clear thickening of the base of the tail in an oblong form, more or less flattened on top. There are similarities with the *Aphaniotis* species.

Keeping: Depending on the species, a rainforest or cloud-forest terraria should be used. The preferred diet of these insectivores must be determined in each case by trial and error.

Range: Altitudes of 0 to about 1800 meters, Borneo and Sumatra.

Literature: Inger, 1960.

Phoxophrys nigrilabris (Peters, 1864)

Description: HBL male 52-54, female 58; TL male 90, female 85 mm. Both sexes have continuous nape and dorsal crests of very small triangular scales. On the occiput and the sides of the head are a few conical scales. Triangular scales on the curve of the eyebrow form a low crest. The back of the body is covered with shingle-shaped scales, keeled at the end, that are mixed with diagonal rows of larger, erect, pointed scales. Only rarely does green coloration with dark, diagonal cross stripes occur. Shades of brownish gray to beige predominate, from which a dark marbling can also stand out. The inside of the mouth is a very dark blue.

Habitat and behavior: *Phoxophrys nigrilabris* lives on trees and bushes of the lowland rainforest. These slow agamids often spend several hours at a time in flowing water. They store the water apparently taken in through the skin and spray it from the cloaca again during the next rain shower. Apparently this behavior is unique among agamids.

Notes: In a not too small rainforest terrarium (H abt. 140, L abt. 80, D abt. 50 cm) the care of this species presents no major problems, even when two males are kept together. They seem to prefer worm-like food such.

Range: Borneo.

Phrynocephalus Kaup, 1825

Toad-headed Agamas: about 38-40 species and 7 subspecies

Characteristics: Toad-heads have a round, blunt-snouted head and a dorsolaterally flattened body without a dorsal crest. They have a gular fold but no gular pouch. Hairlike scales on the eyelids and closable nostrils prevent the entry of sand. The tympanum is covered with scales. On the toes are lateral fringe scales. The dorsal scales are homogeneous or mixed with larger scales. Preanal and femoral pores are absent.

Habits: *Phrynocephalus* species live in arid regions. They prefer sandy expanses, above all dunes, but also live in hard loamy soils and rubble deserts. Through lateral movements of the body, the agamids quickly bury themselves in loose sand. Hibernation takes place from early October to late March. A few species (for example, *Phrynocephalus theobaldi*) are livebearing (ovoviviparous). Smaller species feed principally on ants; larger ones also eat beetles, others insects, and plants.

Keeping: An arid terrarium with dimensions of H abt. 60, L abt. 70, D abt. 50 cm is sufficient for one pair of the smaller species (for larger ones try H abt. 100, L abt. 100, D abt. 60 cm). The substrate must match that of the place of origin. A gnarled branch and a few large rocks serve as decoration. The temperature should exceed 40°C (104°F) in places in the summer and drop to about 20 to 25°C (68 to 77°F) at night. Several species need a larger drop in temperature, and most must be overwintered. Because they do not learn to drink from a water bowl, the terrarium must be sprayed at least every other day. The water should first be enriched with vitamins.

Range: Altitudes of 300-6000 meters, southeastern Europe, Asia Minor, and southwestern to eastern Asia.

Notes: The animals bite readily, which should be kept in mind when handling them.

Literature: Peters, 1984.

Phrynocephalus guttatus guttatus (Gmelin, 1789)
Spotted Toad-head

Description: HBL female up to 65, TL up to 64 mm; hatchlings 22-28 mm in HBL; males are somewhat smaller than females and usually have longer legs and a longer tail. The ventral side is whitish, and the dorsal side of the body is gray, yellowish, or sand-colored to brown. Small dark specks and spots can flow together into a reticulated pattern. The larger yellow specks may be in up to five vertical rows. On the dorsal side of the tail there are conspicuous dark specks; in contrast, the underside is banded in black and white.

Habitat and behavior: The animals live in sandy regions with weedy vegetation. They do not use permanent burrows, but dig new, short burrows in small sand hills that are created in the wind shadow of plants. From October to March the agamids overwinter in burrows 80 to 110 cm (32 to 44 in) deep in the earth. Juveniles eat only insects, but adults also feed on plant parts.

Reproduction: Sexual maturity is reached after a year. From April to mid-August up to three clutches of two or three eggs (8 x 18 mm) are produced. The incubation period is four to six weeks. In the terrarium the female always deposits her eggs in the dampest and coolest places.

Notes: Up to now there have been problems with overwintering because the agamids did not bury themselves as other lizards would normally do. An abbreviated overwintering of about six weeks in a frostfree room kept as cool as possible is nonetheless necessary to stimulate them to breed. With the exception of the first two weeks of overwintering, the terrarium should be lighted for four hours a day. If this is not done, illnesses and losses must be expected. The life expectancy is one to two years in nature, in the terrarium over three years.

Range: *Phrynocephalus guttatus guttatus*—from the northern foothills of the Caucasus Mountains across the northern shore of the Caspian Sea to central Kazakhstan; *Phrynocephalus guttatus kalmykus*—Kazakhstan; *Phrynocephalus guttatus kuschakawitschi*—Jungghariya (Dsungarei).

Literature: Engelmann et al., 1985.

Phrynocephalus mystaceus mystaceus (Pallas, 1776)
Bearded Toad-head

Description: HBL male up to 120, TL up

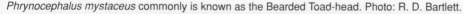

Phrynocephalus mystaceus commonly is known as the Bearded Toad-head. Photo: R. D. Bartlett.

A head study of the Bearded Toad-head, *Phrynocephalus mystaceus*. Notice the "beard" at the corner of the mouth and the curly "eyelashes." Photo: R. D. Bartlett.

to 126 mm, female somewhat smaller; hatchlings 38-43 mm total length. A major characteristic of the species is the presence of folds of skin with spiny scales at the corners of the mouth. When excited they are spread like a beard through the entry of blood. In so doing they turn red and give the impression of a large mouth. The sand-colored back of the lizards is covered with thin black lines that form a fine, irregular network or flow together into dark patches. On the white ventral side is a black breast patch that is somewhat paler in females. The ventral side of the tip of the tail is deep black.

Habitat and behavior: *Phrynocephalus mystaceus* prefers the same biotope as *Phrynocephalus guttatus*. Fleeing lizards cover distances of up to 60 meters (200 ft), pause briefly with rolled-up tail, and sink quickly into loose sand by vibrating the body. Buried in the sand with the nostrils and eyes exposed, the agamids lie in ambush for beetles, other insects, and small lizards. The hibernation period from late September to early April is spent in ground burrows about 180 cm (72 in) long and up to 130 cm (52 in) deep.

Reproduction: *Phrynocephalus mystaceus mystaceus* reaches sexual maturity at two years of age. The breeding season lasts from late April to early July. From the second half of May to late July, older females bury up to two clutches of two or three eggs about 20 cm (8 in) deep in slightly moist sand (in the terrarium up to four clutches of six to nine eggs). The young hatch after 51 to 70 days. Rearing is relatively straightforward.

Notes: When they are exposed to drinking water in a bowl, they fill in the bowl with sand, not recognizing it, apparently, as water. In their natural environment they live to four to six years of age, in the terrarium seven to eight years.

Range: *Phrynocephalus mystaceus mystaceus*—from extreme western Asia and the northern Caucasus along the Caspian Sea across northern Iran and northern Afghanistan to central Asia; *Phrynocephalus mystaceus aurantiacocaudatus* —Kazakhstan.

Literature: Engelmann et al., 1985.

Physignathus Cuvier, 1829

Water Dragons: 2 species

Characteristics: The large water dragons have robust builds and a more or less laterally flattened body that is covered with small scales. They have a gular fold, nape and dorsal crests, a visible tympanum, and femoral pores, but no gular pouch.

Habits: These arboreal agamids live in rainforests and wet forests in the immediate vicinity of water.

Keeping: A large rainforest terrarium (H abt. 140, L abt. 250, D abt. 90 cm) with vertical and diagonal climbing branches is required for a pair. The natural biotope is reproduced by the addition of a rocky landscape. Plantings should not be used, because they do not last long anyway. More than half of the surface area should be made up of an aquatic section about 30 to 40 cm (12 to 16 in) deep. The diet consists of insects, mice, and chicks, with supplements of beef heart, canned dog and cat food, and sweet fruit.

Range: Thailand to southern China; Australia and New Guinea.

Physignathus cocincinus Cuvier, 1829

Green Water Dragon

Description: HBL male 170-250, female 160-200; TL male 480-650 mm, female smaller; hatchlings 45-53 + 86-100 mm (HBL + TL). On the high fold of skin on the nape are separate lanceolate crest

The Brown Water Dragon, here represented by the subspecies *Physignathus lesueuri howitti* from southeastern Australia, recently has been bred in small numbers. Photo: K. H. Switak.

This slender young Brown Water Dragon, *Physignathus lesueuri*, sometimes has been referred to the subspecies *gilberti*, not recognized by most workers. Photo: R. D. Bartlett.

scales. Identical scales are found on the back and the high, strongly flattened front part of the tail. Conspicuously large and often conical scales cover the sides of the lower jaw and the cheeks. These are white, bluish, or reddish to orange. Otherwise nuances of green dominate, with three to five light vertical bars present on the sides. These bars become less distinct with increasing age. Particularly in males, the area of the armpit (axilla) can be yellowish, as can the throat and breast, which, however, can also exhibit shades of green or orange to almost white. The general appearance of the female is altogether more delicate. Her crests are lower, the cheeks do not swell up as much as in the male, the femoral pores are smaller, and the coloration is less intense than that of the male.

Habitat and behavior: *Physignathus cocincinus* is very shy in the wild and always is ready to take flight, sometimes by jumping in the water and escaping by virtue of its swimming and diving skills. Not infrequently this water dragon rests lazily on branches directly over water, but they also spend a lot of time on the ground. At the slightest disturbance they run away on the hind legs with the front legs held close to the body, running until they find cover in dense undergrowth or disappear into larger crevices. Both sexes establish territories that they

defend against intruding conspecifics.

Reproduction: A specific cue for the onset of breeding condition has yet to be found. Several times a year the females bury their 5 to 16 eggs (14-16 x 25-28 mm) about 20 cm (8 in) deep. Just before hatching these reach a size of 17-21 x 30-34 mm. Depending on the incubation temperature (24 to 30°C, 75 to 86°F), the young hatch after 60 to 100 days. With an adequate supply of calcium and vitamins, rearing presents no major problems.

Notes: These agamids can be quite quarrelsome in the terrarium, so no additional water dragons may be added to an existing group. Their nervousness is a big problem. They jump or run against the terrarium glass time and again, which

results in serious injuries to the snout that heal slowly. Therefore, they should be kept only by experienced keepers.

Range: Burma (?) and Thailand to southern China.

Literature: Dedekind & Petzold, 1982.

Physignathus lesueuri lesueuri
(Gray, 1831)

Brown Water Dragon, Australian Water Dragon

Description: HBL 200-250, TL 500-700 mm; hatchlings 146-160 mm in total length. From the occiput almost to the tip

A heavily crested male Green Water Dragon, *Physignathus cocincinus.* Photo: Z. Takacs.

of the tail extends a crest of triangular and serrate scales that are highest on the nape of the male. The rear and side of the head are covered by numerous large, conical scales. Other conical scales run in vertical rows across the back to the belly and are also present on the front part of the tail. The brownish to gray ground color is broken up by black, sometimes rhomboidal dorsal patches or vertical bars. A black band runs from the eye to the shoulder. The ventral side is yellowish to brown (female) or reddish (male).

Habitat and behavior: Brown Water Dragons establish their territories on the banks of cool temperate to subtropical watercourses with stands of trees and bushes. They inhabit the banks of lakes in the mountain chains as well as coastal plains and the wet, rocky coastal plateau of eastern Australia. As adaptable omnivores, they reject neither their own young nor frogs, fishes, crabs, and flowers. For

Green Water Dragons, *Physignathus cocincinus*, are excellent climbers. Large adults need large terraria. Photo: A. Norman.

Though hatchling Green Water Dragons, *Physignathus cocincinus*, can be delicate, they are popular pets. Photo: P. Freed.

Green Water Dragons, *Physignathus cocincinus*, have become popular pets in recent years. If kept warm and humid and fed a variety of fruits and vegetables, they may do very well in captivity. Notice the young *Hydrosaurus* feeding with his green cousins in the top photo. Photos: U. E. Friese.

The Green Water Dragon, *Physignathus cocincinus*, reaches a maximum length of about 90 centimeters. Photo: R. Heselhaus.

An adult Brown Water Dragon, *Physignathus lesueuri*. Photo: Manning.

this reason the juveniles are extremely alert and stay along small tributaries away from the hunting territories of the adults. The diving ability of these agamids is considerable. They can stay under water for up to 90 minutes.

Reproduction: In the Australian spring the females lay 6 to 20 eggs at a distance from their territories. The young hatch after 70 to 120 days. Perhaps more than two clutches per season are possible.

Notes: A short hibernation at daytime

Young Green Water Dragons, *Physignathus cocincinus*, vary considerably in color shade from green to brown or almost black depending on temperature and mood. The oblique pale stripes on the sides are almost always present. Photo: W. P. Mara.

A head study of a young Green Water Dragon, *Physignathus cocincinus*. Notice the lack of the enlarged rounded scale below the angle of the jaw—this scale is present in all Green Iguanas, *Iguana iguana*. The two species often are confused by beginners. Photo: W. P. Mara.

temperatures of about 20°C [68°F] (10 to 15°C [50 to 59°F] at night) seems to be beneficial for successful breeding.

Range: *Physignathus lesueuri lesueuri*—Cape York to central New South Wales, Australia (the New Guinea record appears to be erroneous); *Physignathus lesueuri howitti*—southeastern New South Wales and eastern Victoria, Australia.

Literature: Ehmann, 1992; Smith, 1979.

Pogona **Storr, 1982**

Bearded Dragons: 7 species and 2 subspecies

Characteristics: One of the distinguishing features of the genus is a more or less erectile throat fan ("beard") of spinous scales (with the help of the hyoid or tongue bone). There also are numerous robust spines on the broad, triangular head. The dorsoventrally flattened body is covered with small scales that are always mixed with larger ones. The shoulder has a dark patch and small clusters of spines. Other spiny scales

are arranged in one or more longitudinal rows on the flanks. A dark band usually extends between the eye and tympanum. The plain gray and brown colors of the back show little variation. Males have well-developed hemipenis pouches and their "beard" can turn deep black in color.

Habits: These semi-arboreal agamids inhabit near-deserts, bushy and wooded steppes, as well as open dry forests. Males, in particular, perch on rocks, bushes, or tree stumps to watch over their territory, which is defended stubbornly. They threaten an opponent on the ground by erecting the body, erecting the beard, whipping the tail, opening the mouth wide, and hissing, and also try to drive off the opponent by jumping on it or biting it. Bearded dragons feed on almost any animal small enough for them to overpower, but about half of the diet consists of vegetable matter (leaves, flowers, and fruits).

Keeping: A pair can be housed in an arid terrarium (H abt. 100, L abt. 150, D abt. 80

Bearded dragons, such as this Coastal Bearded Dragon, *Pogona barbata*, display a beard of spiny scales under the throat when annoyed or threatened. Photo: Manning.

cm) with a sandy substrate, rocks as decorations and hiding places, and climbing branches. Temperatures of 30°C (86°F) and locally to 40°C (104°F) under a basking light have proved effective. At night a drop in temperature to at least room temperature is necessary. So that the agamids will go into a short hibernation period, in November and December the heating and some of the lights are switched off. The agamids mate following hibernation in early spring. More than one male cannot be kept in a terrarium because they are extremely quarrelsome.

Range: Australia.

Pogona barbata (Cuvier, 1829)
Coastal Bearded Dragon

Description: HBL male up to 250, TL up to 330 mm; hatchlings 75-100 mm in total length. The well-developed "beard" can be fully erected. The tympanum looks almost triangular. Four rows of spines run across the flanks. The back is dark gray with rhomboidal markings; the pale gray ventral side, in contrast, is marked with ocelli. When excited the head, legs, and flanks turn yellow. *Pogona barbata*

has bright yellow mucous membranes in the mouth. Juveniles have three pale gray spots on the tip of the snout that occasionally run together.

Habitat and behavior: These agamids inhabit cool-temperate to tropical wooded steppes, dry forests, and agricultural lands.

Reproduction: Females reach sexual maturity at a HBL of 130 mm. Four to six weeks after mating, after making a number of test excavations, they lay 18 to 25 eggs (25-30 mm long) in the early evening hours. The incubation period is 63 to 95 days.

Notes: The ravenous youngsters must be divided among several small containers because they quickly form a hierarchy. This is seldom noticed by the keeper, but often leads to the death of the weaker animals because of continual stress.

Range: Eastern Australia, coastal strip from Cooktown to the south. Two isolated populations occur in the southern Mt. Lofty Mountains and on the Eyre Peninsula.

Literature: Badham, 1976; Bustard, 1966.

The dark, black-bearded *Pogona barbata* (above) has been largely replaced in the American terrarium hobby by the smaller, paler *Pogona vitticeps* (below), the Interior Bearded Dragon. Photos: Above: S. Minton; Below: W. P. Mara.

Though bearded dragons such as this *Pogona barbata* usually are gentle animals that will tolerate (and even seem to enjoy) a good deal of handling, they have large teeth and heavy jaw muscles that can produce a good bite it they are pushed too far. Photo: R. D. Bartlett.

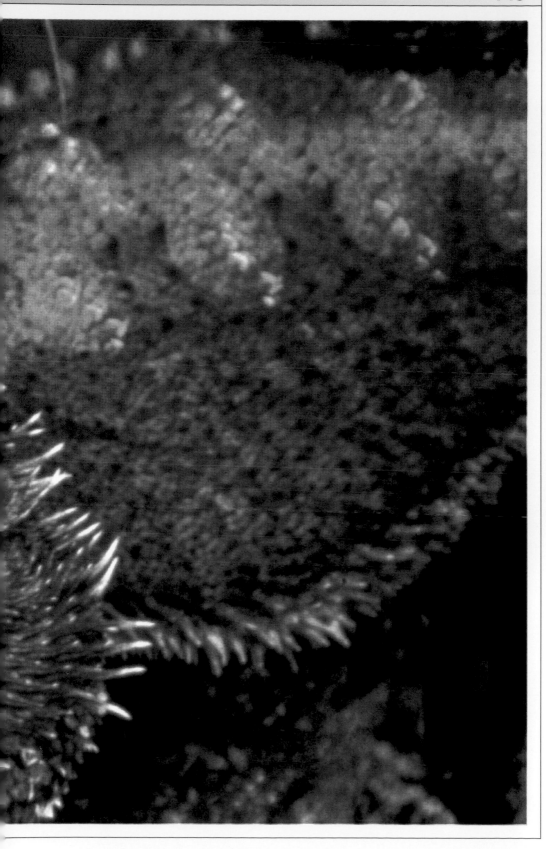

Pogona minor (Sternfeld, 1919)
   Dwarf Bearded Dragon
   Description: HBL female 135, TL 265 mm; hatchlings 65-80 mm in total length. The beard can be erected only slightly and the head is relatively weakly spined. The small tympanum is round. Parallel to the backbone run short rows of spines. The head, legs, and tail are longer and the yellow coloration in good health is less pronounced in *Pogona minor minima* than in *P. m. minor.* The dark gray agamids, with their rhomboidal markings, the light ventral side, and the yellow mucous membranes of the mouth, resemble *Pogona barbata.* During breeding season the males have a black belly.
   Habitat and behavior: Open wooded and bushy landscapes with sandy and rocky soils are favored; in regions near the coast dune landscapes are occupied. In contrast to other bearded dragons, they do not attack an intruder, but rather rely on their camouflage or flee.
   Reproduction: The females, which reach sexual maturity starting at a HBL of 85 mm, lay five to ten eggs. The young hatch after 50 to 63 days. No more than four weeks later they should be separated and reared individually.

Their gentle disposition and calm nature have made bearded dragons, here *Pogona vitticeps,* popular pets. Photo: W. P. Mara.

   Range: *Pogona minor minima*—southwestern Western Australia, Albrolhos and Houtman Islands, as well as West Wallaby Island; *Pogona minor minor*—central Western Australia (including the coast) though central Australia to the Eyre Peninsula, South Australia.
   Literature: Hielscher, 1989.

Pogona mitchelli **(Badham, 1976)**
   Cone-spined Bearded Dragon
   Description: HBL male 155, TL 255 mm, female smaller. The head of these robust agamids, which is about as wide as long, features large scales and an elliptical tympanum. It is equipped with a partially erectile "beard." Males have a larger and more bumpy head than do females. Only one row of spiny scales is present on the sides of the body. In cool weather oval specks appear on both sides of the backbone; otherwise, the animals are brown or sandy yellow to reddish brown with dark markings covering the flanks. The head and tail of excited males turn reddish.
   Habitat and behavior: *Pogona mitchelli* lives in dry forests with tall grass and in desert-like regions on sandy or rocky soils.
   Reproduction: Females are sexually mature at 105 mm HBL. The breeding information is the same as for *Pogona minor.*
   Notes: In the region of overlap in the southern Pilbara region, hybridization occurs between *Pogona mitchelli* and *Pogona minor minor.*
   Range: Northern Western Australia and northwestern Northern Territory.

Pogona nullarbor **(Badham, 1976)**
   Nullarbor Plains Bearded Dragon
   Description: HBL 141, TL 230 mm. The spines on the head are weakly expressed and the beard is only partly erectile. The tympanum has an oval form. *Pogona nullarbor* is considered to be the most colorful agamid. The brown or red to orange-brown back is adorned by six or seven transverse white bars. Greenish gray dorsolateral fields can be present between them. Dark-bordered ocelli stand out from the cream-colored belly and dark stripes contrast with the light gray throat. The inside of the mouth is pink. The short legs and the tail have contrasting crossbanding.

A large adult wild specimen of the Interior Bearded Dragon, *Pogona vitticeps*. Photo: Jakob.

Habitat and behavior: *Pogona nullarbor* lives on calcareous soils with a growth of shrubs, grass, or acacias.

Reproduction: The females reach sexual maturity starting at a HBL of 102 mm. They lay 14 to 19 eggs in October and November. At 27 to 29°C (81 to 84°F), the young hatch in 79 or 80 days.

Range: *Pogona nullarbor* lives in southeastern Western Australia and southwestern South Australia in the region known as the Nullarbor Plain.

Pogona vitticeps (Ahl, 1926)
Interior Bearded Dragon

Description: HBL up to 250, TL up to 310 mm. The fully erectile "beard" is well developed and the head is just as wide as long. The tympanum is oval. On the sides of the body are two orderly rows of spines. The mucous membranes of the mouth are pink. The robust body can be gray, brown, rufus, or yellow, and can exhibit rhomboidal markings. A pattern of ocelli is present on the pale gray belly.

Habitat and behavior: *Pogona vitticeps* prefers a biotope similar to but warmer and drier than that for *Pogona barbata*.

Reproduction: The females are sexually mature at a HBL of 130 mm. They lay two clutches of 11 to 25 eggs starting in October. At 26°C (79°F), the incubation period is 68 to 96 days.

Notes: Males and juveniles are to some extent compatible with one another. As a rule the males establish a hierarchy following each hibernation that is accepted by all until the following season. It is possible to rear several juveniles together. If so, however, the food intake must be controlled and the weaker animals fed separately, if necessary. This currently is the common bearded dragon in the American hobby.

Range: Eastern interior of central Queensland, northern New South Wales to northwestern Victoria, and the eastern half of South Australia and southeastern

The still-undescribed Rankin's Bearded Dragon, *Pogona* sp. Photo: Eidenmueller.

Northern Territory.
Literature: Johnston, 1979; Pflugmacher, 1984.

A male Cone-spined Bearded Dragon, *Pogona mitchelli*. Photo: Eidenmueller.

The Nullarbor Plains Bearded Dragon, *Pogona nullarbor*, is the perhaps the most contrastingly colored species of the genus. Photo: N. Schuster.

Pogona sp.
Rankin's Bearded Dragon

Description: HBL 130, TL 170 mm; hatchlings 55-80 mm in total length. The "beard" and head spines of this, the smallest, shortest-tailed bearded dragon, are only weakly developed. There is a row of spines on the flank. The rather rounded head often exhibits an orange-red speck in the middle of the oval tympanum, as well as a light gray throat irregularly striped with brown, and pale orange mucous membranes in the mouth. The orange-brown body is covered with oval gray patches on both sides of the back-

Pogona minor minima, the Dwarf Bearded Dragon, seldom is available to American hobbyists. Photo: R. D. Bartlett.

A head study of the Interior Bearded Dragon, *Pogona vitticeps*. Photo: J. Merli.

A Rankin's Bearded Dragon, *Pogona* sp., hot on the trail of food. Photo: R. D. Bartlett.

A young adult male Interior Bearded Dragon, *Pogona vitticeps*, from western New South Wales, Australia. Photo: K. H. Switak.

Bearded dragons like these *Pogona vitticeps* are the Australian equivalents of the American horned lizards. Photo: J. Merli.

Top: A captive-bred female Interior Bearded Dragon, *Pogona vitticeps*. Photo: K. H. Switak. Bottom: Bearded dragons like to climb into shrubs and perch to bask in the sun. Photo: U. E. Friese.

Top: The imposing visage of an adult Interior Bearded Dragon, *Pogona vitticeps*. Photo: R. D. Bartlett. Bottom: An Interior Bearded Dragon, *Pogona vitticeps*, from the Gibson Desert of northern Australia. Photo: Z. Takacs.

The Interior Bearded Dragon, *Pogona vitticeps*.
Photo: R. D. Bartlett.

Head studies of the Interior Bearded Dragon, *Pogona vitticeps*. Photos: Above: W. P. Mara; Below: D. J. Zoffer.

The head spines of *Pogona vitticeps* can be imposing to potential predators. Photo: W. P. Mara.

Though large, bearded dragons are easily hand-tamed and often seem to enjoy being handled. This is part of their appeal as pets. Photo: M. & J. Walls.

When a bearded dragon, in this case *Pogona vitticeps*, spreads its beard, the posterior angles of the head also extend, revealing two series of spines. Photo: M. & J. Walls.

Spines on the sides of *Pogona vitticeps* also help give it an impressive profile when it faces off with a predator. Photo: W. P. Mara.

bone, which can run together. Some individuals exhibit scarcely any markings at all. Ocelli often are present on a beige-gray background of the belly and the first two-thirds of the tail.

Habitat and behavior: Rankin's Bearded Dragon lives on a heavy gray-brown substrate, the so-called black-earth soils. The surface is covered with rocks, tufts of grass, and low bushy vegetation. When pursued the lizards disappear into cracks or holes in the soil. Their weak climbing skills agree with a terrestrial existence.

Reproduction: Females lay 8 to 19 eggs from which the young hatch after 50 to 70 days. Unfortunately, this species produces many cripples with rolled-up tails in the terrarium. Apparently such deformities are inherited, so deformed hatchlings should be destroyed, since the damage is irreparable.

Range: Central and western Queensland.

Notes: The species was described in 1985 by Wells & Wellington as *Pogona henrylawsoni*. Because this name was used illegally only in the index, however, the name cannot be used. For more than ten years this agamid has gone by the invalid name "*Amphibolurus rankini*" in the German and American hobby.

Psammophilus Fitzinger, 1843
2 species

Characteristics: The large triangular head without a gular pouch but with a visible tympanum is conspicuous. Small, uniformly arranged scales cover the dorsal side of the dorsoventrally flattened body. On the occiput are small, spiny scales. The nape and dorsal crests are only suggested by tiny triangular scales. Males are distinguished by the clearly visible hemipenis pouches.

Habits: These terrestrial agamids live in rocky landscapes of the highlands. They are said to be extremely active and shy. At the slightest danger they head for safety in the nearest crevice.

Range: India.

Psammophilus blanfordianus Stoliczka, 1871
Indian Sand Agama

Notes: HBL male 100, TL 200 mm, female smaller. The coloration matches that of the rocks in the habitat; males are predominantly brownish with dark markings; juveniles and females are olive-brown, speckled or marbled with brown; large, dark, rhomboidal patches with light centers usually are present on the back and tail. During breeding season (April to May) the front half of male becomes red, the rear half black. An arid terrarium with substantial nocturnal cooling is required. They are basically insectivores. Altitudes of 1300-2100 meters, central and southeastern India.

Literature: Smith, 1935.

Pseudocalotes Fitzinger, 1843
Slender Beauty Lizards: 6 species

Characteristics: The body form shows similarities to the *Calotes* species but appears more slender and delicate. The somewhat variably sized dorsal scales are not as regularly arranged. The head is more elongated, and the legs are as a rule shorter. Isolated scales form a nape crest, and the dorsal crest is only suggested.

Habits: These small agamids probably live on bushes and trees. They seem to prefer the forests of montane regions.

Keeping: In accordance with the altitude of sites where they have been found, rainforest or cloud-forest terraria should be suitable. They feed on insects.

Range: Burma east to southern China, south to Java.

Pseudocalotes tympanistriga (Gray, 1831)

Notes: HBL male 67-80, female 65-68; TL male 157-190, female 145-147 mm; hatchlings 76 mm in total length. The nape crest consists of six or seven small triangular scales; on the back only a row of keeled scales is present over the midline. The rear edge of the curve of the eyebrow has enlarged tubercular scales, and several small spines are present around the tympanum. The shingle-like dorsal scales hardly overlap and are smooth and partially keeled. Both sexes have a gular pouch. Both sexes are green or brownish, with or without dark vertical bars. Two eggs (7.5-8 x 16.5-18 mm) are laid. The incubation period is 70 or 71

days. Approximately 1300-1500 meters, Sumatra and Java.
Literature: Kopstein, 1938.

Pseudotrapelus Fitzinger, 1843
Sinai Agamas: 1 species
Characteristics: *Pseudotrapelus* differs externally from *Trapelus* through its longer legs and larger, more conspicuous ear opening.
Habits: These agamas inhabit lands bordering deserts and feed on insects.
Keeping: See *Trapelus*.
Range: Northeastern Africa and Arabia.

Pseudotrapelus sinaitus (Heyden, 1827)
Sinai Agama
Notes: HBL male 90-100, TL 200 mm; female sexually mature at 75 mm HBL. Back sand-colored, the male's head, body, and front legs blue when excited. Three to nine eggs are laid.

Ptyctolaemus Peters, 1864
2 species
Characteristics: On the throat there are three elongated folds that form a U-shaped figure. The body is laterally or dorsoventrally flattened. Femoral pores can be present, likewise a dorsal crest in males. The tympanum is not visible.
Range: Assam (India), Sizang (Tibet), and northeastern Thailand.

Ptyctolaemus phuwuanensis Manthey & Nabhitabhata, 1991
Description: HBL male 83-86, female 80-83; TL male 182, female 155-164 mm. The head and body are slightly flattened dorsoventrally. The very long extremities feature conspicuously thin, long fingers and toes. The dorsal crest of the male consists of low, triangular scales and is interrupted in the shoulder region. The small, rectangular gular pouch is edged on both sides by three pronounced parallel folds that unite toward the neck in a distinct U. Females have a smaller gular pouch that is rounded on the bottom. In females the dorsal crest is only suggested by a longitudinal row of flat scales. Males are dark brown with greenish spots and light markings on the back. Diagonal rows

of round black specks, which continue to the edge of the belly, are present on the brownish to bluish violet flanks. Between them are pale orange stripes. In the region of the gular pouch the throat is orange-yellow in color and is edged on both sides by two rows each of black, irregularly formed stripes. The lower half of the gular pouch is reddish; in contrast, the belly is bluish violet mixed with yellow. The specks and markings are orange red in the female, whose ventral side is uniformly pale yellow without dark spots.
Habitat and behavior: *Ptyctolaemus phuwuanensis* was found on a flat sandstone hill at altitudes of 200 and 380 meters. This plateau is covered with an evergreen forest, but the slopes feature a dipterocarp dry forest. The agamids inhabit the huge sandstone rocks of the hill, which slopes down to a lake. In late afternoon and at night they seek shelter in narrow crevices or the ceilings of small caves.
Notes: To keep this species, a dry-forest terrarium would have to be modified so that the rear wall is constructed as a rock formation. It can be assumed that these extremely interesting and fast agamids feed on insects.
Range: Phu Wua Wildlife Sanctuary, Nong Khai Province, northeastern Thailand.

Salea Gray, 1845
4 species
Characteristics: The back of the laterally flattened body is covered with roof-tilelike, regularly arranged, but variably sized scales. Both sexes have visible tympana, spiny scales on the occiput, and nape crests. The dorsal crest of the males is at least recognizable anteriorly. In the female, on the other hand, it is more weakly expressed or entirely absent.
Habits: Unfortunately, little information exists about these appealing agamids. They have been observed in trees and on the ground, sometimes actually in the water; they also are followers of civilization in home gardens.
Keeping: Unknown in the terrarium, they probably should be kept in a cloud-forest terrarium with fairly intense light-

ing. They probably feed on insects.

Range: Up to 2400 meters, India, Burma, Thailand, and southwestern China.

Salea kakhienensis is one of several agamids for which there is no information on keeping them in the terrarium. Photo: Nabhitabhata.

Salea horsfieldi Gray, 1845

Notes: HBL male 95, female 75; TL male 250, female 155 mm. Males have interrupted nape and dorsal crests of long, lanceolate scales. The nape crest in females is a double row of short, alternating, slanted scales; the dorsal crest is absent. All the body scales of males are very strongly keeled, in females somewhat more weakly so. Males are exquisitely colored an intense green that becomes yellow toward the head; the gular pouch is bright yellow. Three or four eggs (9 x 17 mm) are laid. These agamids live in bushes, hedges, and gardens and might do well in a cloud-forest terrarium. Altitudes of 1800-240 meters, Nilgiri and Plani Hills, southern India.

Literature: Smith, 1935.

Salea kakhienensis (Anderson, 1878)

Notes: HBL male 94-125, female 83; TL male 176-255, female 141 mm. The nape crest consists of elongated triangular scales; the dorsal crest comprises very short, triangular scales (males) or is scarcely discernible (females). Two or three spines are present between the tympanum and nape crest. The male has a broad head and conspicuous hemipenis pouches. Both sexes are light greenish to pale tan with dark speckling and alternating lighter and darker broad vertical bands. Five eggs are laid. These agamas are arboreal or terrestrial depending on where they are found and may even enter the water. A cloud-forest terrarium with a large surface area might work to keep these lizards. Mountainous regions from Burma through northern Thailand to western Yunnan, China.

Literature: Smith, 1935.

Sitana Cuvier, 1829

Four-toed Agamas: 1 species

Characteristics: A single character is sufficient to distinguish *Sitana* from all other agamid genera: the feet have only four toes.

Habits: Although the laterally flattened body points to an arboreal way of life, this agamid stays predominantly on the ground and in low bushes. It inhabits sparsely vegetated arid zones of the lowlands.

Keeping: In a fairly large arid terrarium (H abt. 100, L abt. 150, D abt. 60 cm) with a sandy substrate and a few bushy plants, the behavior of one male and two females can be observed well. During the day they need a relative humidity of 50 to 70 percent and local substrate and air temperatures (under the basking light) of up to 45°C (115°F); the rest of the terrarium can be kept at 30 to 35°C (86 to 95°F), reduced at night to 22 to 28°C (72 to 82°F).

The only member of its genus, *Sitana ponticeriana*, the Four-toed Agama, is a common Indian and Sri Lankan species that seldom enters the terrarium market. Photo: Forman.

Range: Sri Lanka and India east to the Ganges.

Sitana ponticeriana Cuvier, 1829
Four-toed Agama
Description: HBL both sexes 70-80, TL up to 160 mm (vicinity of Bombay); HBL male 42-57, female 36-52, TL up to 150 mm (rest of India and Sri Lanka); hatchlings 17 + 32 mm (HBL + TL). This agamid has a visible tympanum, but the nape and dorsal crests are absent. A pattern of dark brown black-edged rhomboidal patches runs along the light middorsal longitudinal band. The remainder of the back is brownish with scattered darker or lighter patches. The inside of the mouth is blue. The males are easy to recognize by the huge gular pouch, which reaches to the belly, and the brilliant color that displays during breeding season: the orange or pink center has a pale yellow or whitish border, the lilac-blue of the keel standing in bright contrast.

Habitat and behavior: Four-toed Agamas sunbathe on the hot sand even in the heat of midday. When threatened, they run rapidly on two legs with raised tail to the nearest hole in the ground or to a hiding place. They rarely live more than one year, because too many predators, among others *Calotes* species, lie in wait for them in their habitat.

Reproduction: Matings take place in southeastern India between April and September. From June through August to October, following rains, females lay eggs (6 x 9-10 mm) once or several times in self-excavated holes. In Sri Lanka, clutches number six to eight eggs; in the vicinity of Poona (India) 11 to 14; and at Tirupati (India) 8 to 13 eggs were laid. After an incubation period of 42 or 43 days, the first youngsters appear in October. Hatching takes about four to five hours. The agamids are sexually mature at the latest in March of the following year.

Notes: *Sitana ponticeriana* feeds primarily on termites (65 percent), red ants (25 percent), and other small insects.

Literature: Chopra, 1964; Deraniyagala, 1953; Rao & Rajabai, 1972a, b.

Thaumatorhynchus Parker, 1924
1 species
Characteristics: As with *Harpesaurus*, a visible tympanum and a hornlike frontal appendage are present. The fairly small dorsal scales, however, are rounded.

Habits: Possibly similar to *Harpesaurus* and *Ceratophora.*

Keeping: Because this species is found in the mountains, a cloud-forest terrarium would seem to be a good first choice until

Steppes agamas, *Trapelus* sp., usually lack bright colors, making it easier for them to disappear into the sand. Photo: R. D. Bartlett.

A head study of a male steppes agama, *Trapelus* sp. Photo: R. D. Bartlett.

more experience has been gained. These rare agamids probably eat insects.

Range: Sumatra.

Thaumatorhynchus brooksi Parker, 1924

Notes: HBL male 60, TL 140 mm. The nape crest consists of seven separately arranged, small lanceolate scales; the dorsal crest is only suggested by slightly enlarged scales. A small gular pouch is visible. These arboreal agamids primarily exhibit shades of brown interspersed with green. Lebongtandai, Rejanglebong District, Bengkulu, Sumatra.

Trapelus Cuvier, 1816

Steppes Agamas: About 11 species and 6 subspecies

Characteristics: The somewhat conical head with a small tympanum calls to mind *Phrynocephalus*. The body is weakly flattened dorsoventrally and has homogeneous or heterogeneous scalation. The roof-tilelike caudal scales run in diagonal rows and are not arranged in obliquely segmented whorls. The predominantly gray-brown ground color can change quickly to brighter colors. Males have horny preanal scales and a fairly long tail.

Habits: *Trapelus* species live in deserts and steppes with different kinds of soils and sparse vegetation. In some regions the agamids are found at altitudes of up to 1100 meters. When threatened they take refuge in holes in the soil, under clumps of plants, or rely on their mimicry. Their diet is principally made up of insects, but plants also are eaten. The lizards hibernate in winter for periods of varying length.

Keeping: An arid terrarium with the dimensions H abt. 100, L abt. 120, D abt. 80 cm is adequate for a pair. The substrate of sand or sand and loam can be decorated with fairly large rocks, a climbing branch, and a few succulents. The temperature range during the day should be between 25°C (77°F) and locally 40°C (104°F) under the basking light, dropping at night to about 20°C (68°F).

Range: The genus *Trapelus* is found from extreme southeastern Europe along the Caspian Sea to southwestern Asia (Pakistan) and south across Asia Minor and the Arabian Peninsula to North Africa (Egypt to Morocco).

Trapelus sanguinolentus sanguinolentus (Pallas, 1814)
Steppes Agama

Description: HBL male 118, female 118; TL male 236, female 178 mm; hatchlings 29-38 mm HBL. The uniform roof-tilelike dorsal scales are equipped with keels that end in a spine. Males have two rows of preanal pores. Their often unmarked back is yellowish gray. Females and juveniles have pale, oval, dark-edged rows of specks on the back. Besides an intense change in color in response to changes in temperature or other external influences, males exhibit an almost blue-black, lightly striped throat during the breeding season. The breast and flanks then turn intense dark violet, the legs change to blue, and the tail takes on a yellow-orange cross-banding. The back and top of the head turn light yellow to beige. Females in breeding condition exhibit orange to rust-red dorsal specks on the bluish to greenish yellow back.

Habitat and behavior: These terrestrial agamids inhabit steppes as well as semi-arid locations. They sometimes climb around in the weedy and shrubby vegetation. Sandy soils are preferred, but they also colonize fields of rubble in mountainous areas as well as cultivated landscapes. Sometimes a pair stays together for a fairly long time and defends a territory. From October to March (in the terrarium from November to January), the lizards take refuge in holes and rodent dens to hibernate.

Reproduction: Steppes Agamas mate between April and June. Two to four clutches, each with 6 to 12 eggs, are produced each season. The incubation period is 50 to 60 days. The youngsters must be reared in small groups or individually, because they are very aggressive. They are sexually mature after just one year.

Characteristics: Unfortunately, Steppes Agamas are always somewhat delicate in the indoor terrarium. Therefore, they should only be kept when outdoor terraria are available. It should be kept in mind that females also need their own territory.

Range: *Trapelus sanguinolentus aralensis*—area around the Sea of Aral; *Trapelus sanguinolentus sanguinolentus*—from eastern Caucasus through Kazakhstan and all of central Asia to northwestern China, southern limit through northwestern Iran and northern Afghanistan.

Tympanocryptis Peters, 1863
Deaf Agamas: 10 species and 5 subspecies

Characteristics: In five species the tympanum is absent, and in the other five it is more or less hidden by scales. These small, blunt-snouted terrestrial agamids have a short tail and, of all Australian agamids, the shortest legs. Dorsal and nape crests are absent. The dorsoventrally flattened body often exhibits camouflage coloration with dark as well as light specks or stripes or both. In contrast to the sometimes plain female, the colors and markings of the male appear richer. Males have more or less pronounced hemipenis pouches; a few species even have dark ventral markings.

Habits: *Tympanocryptis* species inhabit rocky and sandy deserts as well as open wooded and scrubby landscapes with rocky or stony soils. These agamids only become truly active at high temperatures. Though females are hard to find, males often perch in exposed places. When threatened they disappear into cracks under rocks or in holes in the ground; others remain motionless and rely on their camouflage. They feed on small insects; a few species prefer ants.

Keeping: For one pair, an arid terrarium (H abt. 60, L abt. 80, D abt. 50 cm) with loamy sand, large and small rocks, and a gnarled branch is sufficient. As a dietary supplement, vegetables should be offered occasionally.

Range: Australia.

Tympanocryptis lineata lineata Peters, 1863

Description: HBL 68, TL 92 mm. Males are gray, brown, or orange-brown and are distinguished by light vertebral and dorsolateral stripes that can be broken up by vertical bars or spots. The ventral side has dark markings. Females are plain,

Tympanocryptis diemensis, a deaf agama collected in New South Wales, Australia. Photo: R. W. Van Devender.

When warm, the African Uromastyx, *Uromastyx acanthinurus*, can be a very colorful lizard. Photo: P. Freed.

with weakly suggested longitudinal stripes and a conspicuously cross-banded tail.

Habitat and behavior: This subspecies inhabits regions with open vegetation and rocky soils.

Reproduction: Little is known, but 9 to 11 eggs are laid.

Notes: These agamids soon lose their shyness in the terrarium.

Range: *Tympanocryptis lineata centralis*—central Australia; *Tympanocryptis lineata houstoni*—Nullarbor Plain; *Tympanocryptis lineata macra*—arid region of Kimberley and the Northern Territory; *Tympanocryptis lineata pinguicolla*—vicinity of Melbourne; *Tympanocryptis lineata lineata*—remainder of central Australia.

Uromastyx Merrem, 1820

Uromastyx, Mastigures, Spiny-tailed Agamas: 14 species, 6 subspecies

Characters: The short tail with sharp whorls as well as a strongly flattened body with short, powerful legs produces a distinctive appearance. The head, which lacks a gular pouch and is clearly set off from

the neck, has a visible tympanum and a gular fold. Preanal and femoral pores can be present or absent.

Habits: Uromastyx live in sandy regions, rocky deserts, and plains with sparse vegetation. They are highly specialized for very arid habitats. At least a few species resorb water from their excrement, use the water produced through the oxidation of the fat reserves in the tail, or both. When threatened and at night spiny-tails disappear into crevices or crawl through deep burrows to a small den. Though adults feed almost exclusively on plants, juveniles also take insects. Northern species hibernate.

Keeping: For one male and two females, an arid terrarium (H abt. 100, L abt. 150, D abt. 80 cm) with a layer of sand and loam 50 to 80 cm (20 to 32 in) deep is suitable. Several stone slabs well-anchored to each other complete the interior furnishing. High daytime temperatures of 25°C (77°F) to locally (under a basking light) as high as 50°C (122°F), with a nocturnal decrease to 20 to 24°C (68 to 75°F), are necessary. A drinking bowl is not necessary, since the

A head study of *Uromastyx acanthinurus*. Photo: R. D. Bartlett.

Some *Uromastyx acanthinurus* adapt quickly to the terrarium. Photo: W. Schmidt.

Portrait of *Uromastyx acanthinurus*. Photo: Forman.

required water is taken in with the food. Only the hiding place should be kept slightly damp through spraying. The climatic conditions of the native range should be determined if possible and the diet adapted accordingly. For example, leafy vegetables, herbs, yellow and red flowers, and pieces of apple should be offered only during or shortly after the rainy period; in the dry season, in contrast, only dry leaves, seeds, and legumes should be fed.

The African Uromastyx, *Uromastyx acanthinurus*, once was exported from Morocco in large numbers for the European terrarium hobby. Photo: U. E. Friese.

Seldom imported, the Arabian *Uromastyx benti* is one of two species in the genus that lacks femoral pores. Photo: R. D. Bartlett.

Notes: The eggs must be kept just barely damp during incubation.

Range: From Morocco to Egypt across the Arabian Peninsula to northwestern India, and to the south through the Sudan to Somalia.

Uromastyx acanthinurus (Bell, 1825) African Uromastyx

Description: HBL male 220, TL 183 mm, female somewhat smaller; hatchlings 69-78 mm in total length. The tail, with 17 to 20 robust, thorny rows of whorls, is just as strongly flattened dorsoventrally as the wrinkled body. The ground color varies from light to dark gray to brownish and has variable dark speckling, marbling, or netting. The head, legs, and ventral side can be black. At high temperatures the back turns light to dark green or yellow to orange. Often males can only be recognized by their occasionally reddish heads, because the hemipenis pouches are only weakly developed. Their preanal pores are enlarged during courtship.

Habitat and behavior: *Uromastyx acanthinurus acanthinurus* inhabits veg- etation-poor sandy and stony regions of the high valleys and plains, as well as oases and isolated mountains in the desert where the morning dew supports sparse vegetation. When threatened they disappear into their self-excavated burrows or into crevices, where they wedge themselves by inflating the body and defend themselves by lashing their tail. Particularly during the breeding season, males mark their territories through elaborate movements known as the spinning dance.

Reproduction: Copulations begin about a month after hibernation (mid-November to mid-February) at 12 to 18°C (54 to 65°F) or room temperature. Females often bury their 5 to 16 eggs (20 x 36 mm) under a flagstone. The youngsters hatch after 86 to 123 days and take their first food two to five days later.

Notes: The lizards soon become trusting, but can drive the keeper to despair through their digging.

Range: *Uromastyx acanthinurus acanthinurus*—northwestern Africa; *Uromastyx acanthinurus dispar*—the Sudan; *Uromastyx acanthinurus flavifasciatus*—Senegal; *Uromastyx*

The very plainly colored *Uromastyx aegypticus*, like all the other species of the genus, requires hot, dry terraria and a varied vegetarian diet to thrive. Photo: M. Panzella.

Uromastyx aegypticus. Photo: K. H. Switak.

Young specimens of *Uromastyx aegypticus* are only a bit more colorful than adults. Photos: Above: P. Freed; Below: K. H. Switak.

Uromastyx aegypticus is well-adapted to life in the desert. The large nostrils hide a gland that removes excess salt from the system. Darkly colored individuals are cool and need to bask. Photos: K. H. Switak.

The small (under 30 cm) and colorful *Uromastyx ocellatus* is a member of a group of several very similar species that may be imported in large numbers. Photo: A. Norman.

acanthinurus geyri—Hoggar and Ahaggar Mountains, central Sahara; *Uromastyx acanthinurus nigerrimus*—southern part of the Algerian Sahara; *Uromastyx acanthinurus werneri*—western Algeria to Morocco.

Literature: Ortner, 1989a, b.

Uromastyx hardwicki Gray, 1827
Indian Uromastyx

Description: HBL male 168-240, female 145-207; TL male 130-200 mm, female shorter. Indian Uromastyx are easy to recognize by the small, rather conical head. Their coloration varies from khaki and brownish to sand-colored, in part with a fine dark netting. A black patch is located on the thigh. The belly is lighter and the throat has dark spots. A few populations have spiny turquoise scales on the top of the ten anterior tail segments. The body of the brownish juvenile is covered with black spots, but the head and shoulders are speckled with white.

Habitat and behavior: These spiny-tails inhabit flat deserts and steppe-like landscapes with bushy euphorbias, nightshades, and dry grasses. In some regions they live in colonies of 50 to 100 individuals. Each animal excavates in the loamy to sandy, rock-strewn soil a burrow that runs diagonally downward to a depth of up to 76 cm (30 in). The passages, which usually have at least one right-angle bend, end after 60 to 125 cm (24 to 50 in) in a club-shaped chamber that never contains droppings or food remains. As long as the sky is not completely overcast, the agamids leave their dens two hours after sunrise and do not return until one hour before sunset. They overwinter in their dens from November to February.

Reproduction: The breeding season begins in March shortly after the end of hibernation. From late April to June the females lay their clutches of 8 to 14 oval (25-30 mm long) eggs. The first young hatch in late June.

Range: Altitudes of 0-450 meters, Pa-

Uromastyx hardwicki. Photo: Grossmann.

Baby Indian Uromastyx, *Uromastyx hardwicki*, are appealing little lizards, but they can be very hard to keep in the terrarium. Photo: M. & J. Walls, courtesy Adam's Pet Safari.

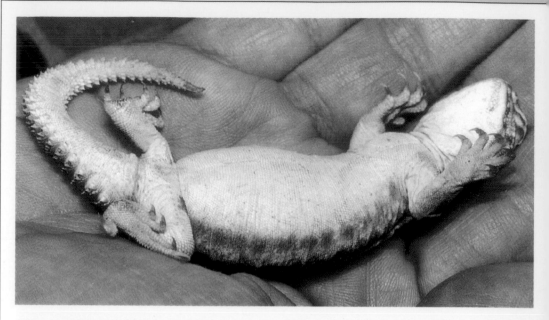

Above and Below Left: The Indian Uromastyx, *Uromastyx hardwicki*, has small spines on the tail in many whorls. Today it is an uncommon import. Keep them hot and dry for success. Photos: M. & J. Walls, courtesy Adam's Pet Safari. Below Right: In the colorful *Uromastyx ornatus* and most other uromastyx species, both sexes have prominent pores on the back of the thigh, the femoral pores. Photo: W. P. Mara.

The Ornate Uromastyx, *Uromastyx ornatus*, may be the most commonly imported uromastyx at the moment in the United States. Though colorful and gentle, it seldom has been bred in the terrarium. Photos: W. P. Mara.

If fed insects and other animal proteins, uromastyx such as *Uromastyx ornatus* may suffer kidney problems. Feed them on a wide variety of fruits and vegetables, not just lettuce. Photos: W. P. Mara.

kistan and the Indian provinces of Uttar Pradesh, Rajastan, and Gujarat.
Literature: Minton, 1966; Schroeder, 1965.

Xenagama Loveridge, 1942
2 species
Characteristics: The extremely short tail with its robust whorled scales is unique among agamids. The base of the tail has a greatly widened, flat form, while the posterior half looks rounded and very slender. These small terrestrial agamids have a dorsoventrally flattened body; the head has a visible tympanum and a gular fold.
Habits: Unknown.
Range: Somalia.

Xenagama batillifera (Vaillant, 1882)
Notes: HBL 65, TL 30 mm (broadest part of tail 15 mm). The legs are very short. Small dorsal scales are mixed with larger ones. The body is pale with dark vertical bands, and the throat has reticulate markings.

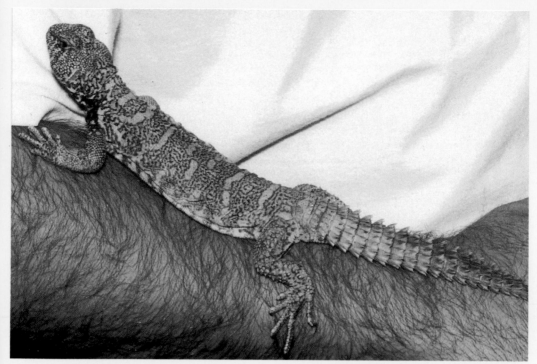

Above: The rings of heavy spines around the tail of *Uromastyx ornatus* and related species have given them the common name of spiny-tailed agamids. Similar tails are found in many American iguanids, examples of parallel evolution. Photo: W. P. Mara.

Below: Several species of uromastyx rarely are available in the hobby. One such is the Arabian *Uromastyx microlepis*. Photo: K. H. Switak.

Bibliography

Abraham, G. 1983. Terrarienbau und Gestaltung—Deko-Felsen im Eigenbau. *Sauria, Berlin,* 5(3): 29-32.

Annandale, N. 1912. Eggs and young of the lizard *Calotes nigrilabris. Spolia Zeylanica,* 24(3): 135-136.

Ax, P. 1984. *Das Phylogenetische Syste.* G. Fischer, Stuttgart. 349 pp.

Badham, J. A. 1976. The *Amphibolurus barbatus* species-group. *Aust. J. Zool.,* 24: 424-443.

Beutler, A. 1981. In Boehme, W. *Handbuch der Reptilien und Amphibien Europas.* Akad. Verlagsges., Wiesbaden. 520 pp.

Boehme, W. 1989. Rediscovery of the Sumatran agamid lizard *Harpesaurus beccarii* Doria 1888, with the first notes on a live specimen. *Tropical Zool.,* 2: 31-35.

Bosch, H. 1991. Erkrankungen von Leguanen, Vorbeugung und Behandlung. In Bosch, H. & H. Werning: *Leguane.* Herp. Fachverlag, Muenster, pp. 14-26.

Bustard, H. R. 1966. Notes on eggs, incubation and young of the Bearded Dragon, *Amphibolurus barbatus barbatus. Brit. J. Herpet.,* 3(10): 252-259.

Chopra, R. N. 1964. Observations on the egg-laying of the fanthroated lizard, *Sitana ponticeriana* Cuvier. *J. Bombay Nat. Hist. Soc.,* 61(1): 190-191, 2 pls.

Daniel, J. C. 1983. *The Book of Indian Reptiles.* Oxford Univ. Press, Bombay. 141 pp.

Dedekind, K. & H.-G. Petzold. 1982. Zur Haltung und Nachzucht der hinterindischen Wasseragame (*Physignathus cocincinus* [Cuvier, 1829]) im Tierpark Berlin. *Zool. Garten N.F., Jena,* 52(1): 29-45.

Deraniyagala, P. E. P. 1953. *A Colored Atlas of Some Vertebrates From Ceylon. Vol. II: Tetrapod Reptilia.* Ceylon Govt. Press, Colombo. 35 pp, 11 pls.

Ehmann, H. 1992. *Encyclopedia of Australian Animals. Reptiles.* Angus & Robertson, Australia. 495 pp.

Engelmann, W.-E., R. Fritsche, R.

Guenther & F. J. Obst. 1985. *Lurche und Kriechtiere Europas.* Neumann, Radebeul. 420 pp.

Erdelen, W. 1984. The genus *Calotes* (Sauria, Agamidae) in Sri Lanka, distribution patterns. *J. et Biogeography,* 11: 515-525.

Gaulke, M. 1989. Einige Bemerkungen uber die philippinische Segelechse *Hydrosaurus pustulatus* (Eschscholtz, 1829). *herpetofauna, Weinstadt,* 11(62): 6-12.

Hielscher, M. 1989. Haltung und Nachzucht der australischen Zwergbartagame *Pogona minima. Elaphe,* 11(2): 21-24.

Houston, T. F. 1974. Revision of the *Amphibolurus decresii*-complex in South Australia. *Trans. Roy. Soc. S. Aust.,* 98: 49-60.

Inger, R. F. 1983. Morphological and ecological variation in the flying lizards (genus *Draco*). *Fieldiana Zool., Chicago,* new series, 18:1-35,

Ippen, R., H.-D. Schroeder & K. Elze. 1985. *Handbuch der Zootierkrankheiten. Bd. 1, Reptilien.* Akad.-Verlag, Berlin, 432 pp.

Jamdar, N. 1985. A note on the habits and breeding of the lizard, *Japalura major* (Jerdon). *J. Bombay Nat. Hist. Soc.,* 82: 420-421.

Johnston, G. R. 1979. The eggs, incubation and young of the Bearded Dragon *Amphibolurus vitticeps. Herpetofauna, Victoria,* 11(1): 5-8.

Kaestle, W. 1966. Beobachtungen an ceylonesischen Taubagamen (*Cophotis ceylanica*). *Salamandra, Frankfurt/M.,* 2(3): 78-87.

Kiehlmann, D. 1980. Uber die Lyrakopfagamen, *Lyriocephalus scutatus* (Linnaeus, 1758). *herpetofauna, Ludwigsburg,* 2(8): 12-120.

King, W. 1982. A new Bornean lizard of the genus *Harpesaurus. Sarawak Mus. J., Kuching,* 307: 205-209.

Klage, H. G. 1982. Pflege und Nachzucht der australischen Bodenagame *Amphibolurus nuchalis. Salamandra,*

Frankfurt/M., 18(1/2): 65-70.

Kopstein, F. 19xx. *Zoologische Tropenreise. Mit Kamera und Feldstecher durch die Indo-Australische Tierwelt.* G. Kolff & Co., Batavia. 163 pp.

—1938. Ein Beitrag zur Eierkunde und Fortpflanzung der malaiischen Reptilien. *Bull. Raffles Mus., Singapore,* 14: 81-167.

Krasula, K. 1988. Haltung und Zucht der Segelesche *Hydrosaurus pustulatus. herpetofauna, Weinstadt,* 10(53): 30-34.

Lazell, J. 1992. New flying lizards and predictive biogeography of two Asian archipelagos. *Bull. Mus. Comp. Zool., Harvard,* 152(9): 475-505.

Leviton, A. E., S. C. Anderson, K. Adler & S. A. Minton. 1992. *Handbook to Middle East Amphibians and Reptiles.* SSAR, Oxford, Ohio. 252 pp. (*Contr. Herp. No. 8*)

Manning, A. 1991. Notes on the nesting, incubation and hatching of the southern angle-headed dragon, *Hypsilurus spinipes* (Squamata, Agamidae). *Herpetofauna, Victoria,* 21(2): 15-19.

—& H. Ehmann. 1991. A study of the activity and behaviour of the southern angle-headed dragon using the spool tracking technique. *Herpetofauna, Victoria,* 21(1): 5-14.

Manthey, U. 1979. Terrarienbau und -gestaltung. -Planung. *Sauria, Berlin,* 2(1): 26-30. Series of 10 articles on topic, all in *Sauria, Berlin,* from 1979 to 1983:

1980a, 2(2): 23-27.
1980b, 2(3): 25-32.
1980c, 2(4): 7-10.
1981a, 3(1): 27-34.
1981b, 3(2): 12-14.
1981c, 3(3): 33-34.
1981d, 3(4): 29-34.
1982, 4(1): 31-33.
1983, 5(3): 21-28.

—& W. Denzer. 1982. Exkursion am Mt. Kinabalu 4100 m, Nord-Borneo. Tiel 2. Herpetologische Eindruecke. *Herpetofauna, Weinstadt,* 4(21): 11-19.

—1985a. *Calotes versicolor* (Daudin). *Sauria, Berlin,* 7(1): A&R Kartei: 3-6.

—1985b. *Otocryptis wiegmanni* Wagler. Ibid, 7(2): A&R Kartei: 11-12.

—1990. *Harepsaurus beccarii* Doria. Ibid, 12(3): 1-2.

—& Denzer, 1991a. Die Echten Winkelkopfagamen der Gattung *Gonocephalus* Kaup (Sauria: Agamidae). I. Die *megalepis*-Gruppe mit *Gonocephalus lacunosus* sp. n. aus Nord-Sumatra. Ibid, 13(1): 3-10.

—& 1991b. dto. II. Allgemeine Angaben zur Biologie und Terraristik. Ibid, 13(2): 19-22.

—& 1991c. dto. III. *Gonocephalus grandis* (Gray, 1845). Ibid, 13(3): 3-10.

—& 1992a. dto. IV. *Gonocephalus mjoebergi* Smith, 1925 und *Gonocephalus ronisonii* Boulenger, 1908. Ibid, 14(1): 15-19.

—& 1992b. dto. V. Die *bellii*-Gruppe. Ibid, 14(3): 20.

—& 1992c. dto. VI. Die *chamaeleontinus*-Gruppe. Ibid, 14(4).

—& J. Nabhitabhata. 1991. Eine neue Agame, *Phyctolaemus phuwuanensis* sp. n. (Sauria: Agamidae) aus Nordost-Thailand. Ibid, 13(4): 3-6.

Matt, F. von. 1984. *Zimmergewaechshaus- und Pflanzenvitrinenbau.* Dt. Bromelienges, Frankfurt/M. 201 pp.

Mayr, E. 1975. *Grundlagen der zoologischen Systematik.* Paul Parrey, Hamburg/Berlin. 370 pp.

McCoy, M. 1980. *Reptiles of the Solomon Islands.* Wau Ecology Inst. Handbook No. 7. 80 pp.

Mell, R. 1952. Bodenrenner im subtropischen Bergwald. Der Nackenstachler (*Gonocephalus lepidogaster*). *DATZ, Stuttgart,* 5(6): 160-163.

Minton, S. A. 1966. A contribution to the herpetology of West Pakistan. *Bull. Amer. Mus., New York,* 143(2): 29-134, 36 pls.

Moody, S. M. 1980. Phylogenetic and historical biogeographical relationship of the genera in the family Agamidae (Reptilia: Lacertilia). Ph.D. Thesis, Univ. Michigan, Ann Arbor. 373 pp.

Musters, C. J. M. 1983. Taxonomy of the genus *Draco* L. (Agamidae, Lacertilia, Reptilia). *Zool. Verh. Leiden,* 199: 120.

Ortner, A. 1989a. Pflegebedingungen und Nachzucht der Nordafrikanischen Dortnschwanzagame (*Uromastyx acanthinurus* Bell, 1825). *herpetofauna, Weinstadt*, 11(59): 11-16.

—1989b. Widerholte Nachzucht der Nordafrikanischen Dornschwanzagame (*Uromastyx acanthinurus* Bell, 1825). Ibid, 11(63): 20-21.

Ota, A. 1991. Systematics and biogeography of terrestrial reptiles of Taiwan. *Proc. First Int. Symp. Wildlife Cons., ROC, Taipei,*: 47-112.

Peters, G. 1971. Die intragenerischen Gruppen und die Phylogenese der Schmetterlingsagamen (Agamidae: *Leiolepis*). *Zool. Jb. Syst., Jena*, 98: 11-130.

—1984. Die Kroetenkopfagamen Zentralasiens (Agamidae: *Phrynocephalus*). *Mitt. zool. Mus. Berlin*, 60(1): 23-67.

Pianka, E. R. 1971. Notes on the biology of *Amphibolurus cristatus* and *Amphibolurus scutulatus*. *W. Aust. Nat.*, 12: 36-41.

Pflugmacher, S. 1984. Haltung und Zucht der Australischen Bartagame *Amphibolurus vitticeps* Loveridge, 1934. *Sauria, Berlin*, 6(3): 9-11.

Pope, C. H. 1935. *The Reptiles of China*. Natural History of Central Asia, Vol. 10. Amer. Mus. Nat. Hist., New York. 603 pp.

Prinz, H. & T. Prinz. 1986. Beobachtungen an der Lyrakopfagame (*Lyriocephalus scutatus*), ihre Haltung und Aufzucht. *herpetofauna, Weinstadt*, 8(43): 28-34.

Rao, M. V. S. & B. S. Rajabai. 1972a. Reproduction in the ground lizard, *Sitana ponticeriana*, and the garden lizard, *Calotes nemoricola*. *Brit. J. Herp.*, 4(10): 245-250.

—& 1972b. Ecological aspects of the agamid lizards *Sitana ponticeriana* and *Calotes nemoricola* in India. *Herpetologica*, 28(3): 285-289.

Rooij, N. de. 1915. *The reptiles of the Indo-Australian Archipelago. I. Lacertilia, Chelonia, Emydosauria.* E. J. Brill, Leiden. 384 pp.

Schroeder, W. 1965. Ueber die Lebensweise des Indischen Dornschwanze. *Sitz. Ber. Ges. Naturf. Freunde Berlin*, 4(2): 39-43.

Senanayake, F. R. 1979. Notes on the lizards of the genus *Ceratophora*. *Loris, Colombo*, 15(1): 18-19.

Sengoku, S. 1979. *Amphibien und Reptilien in Farbe*. 206 pp. (In Japanese)

Smith, J. 1979. Notes on incubation and hatching of eggs of the eastern water dragon. *Herpetofauna, Victoria*, 10(2): 12-14.

Smith, M. A. 1935. *The Fauna of British India, Ceylon and Burma. Reptilia and Amphibia. Vol. II. Sauria.* Taylor & Francis, London. 440 pp.

Steiof, C., U. Manthey & W. Denzer. 1991. *Acanthosaura armata* (Hardwicke & Gray). *Sauria, Berlin*, 13(1-4) SUPPL., 217-222.

Stejneger, L. 1907. Herpetology of Japan and adjacent territory. *Bull. U.S. Nat. Mus.*, 58: 577 pp.

Taylor, E. H. 1922. *The Lizards of the Philippine Islands*. Bur. Printing, Manila. 269 pp.

—1922-1925. Additions to the herpetological fauna of the Philippine Islands. I. pp. 161-206; II. pp. 257-303; III. pp. 515-555; IV. pp. 97-111. Bur. Printing, Manila.

—1951. Egg-laying behavior of an Oriental agamid lizard. *Herpetologica*, 7(2): 59-60.

—1963. The lizards of Thailand. *Univ. Kansas Sci. Bull.*, 44: 687-1077.

Tomey, W. A. 1983a. Von Stachelnasen, Stumpfnasen und Spitznasen—Agamen von Sri Lanka (Ceylon). I. *Das Aquarium*, 167: 268-272.

—1983b. dto. II. Ibid, 168: 321-326.

Ulber, T., W. Grossmann, J. Beutelschiess & C. Beutelschiess. 1989. *Terraristisch/ Herpetologisches Fachwoerterbuch*. Berlin. 176 pp.

Visser, G. 1984. Husbandry and reproduction of the sail-tailed lizard, *Hydrosaurus amboinensis* (Schlosser, 1768) (Reptilia: Sauria: Agamidae), at Rotterdam Zoo. *Acta Zool. Path., Antverpen*, 78: 129-148.

Wegner, U. 1990. Kaukasusagamen (*Stellio caucasia* Eichwald, 1831) im Terrarium. *Sauria, Berlin*, 12(2): 7-9.

Wermuth, H. 1967. Liste der rezenten Amphibien und Reptilien: Agamidae. *Das Tierreich, Berlin*, 86: 127 pp.

TEXT INDEX

INDEX TO PHOTOS